How To Sex Cage Birds: British and Foreign

by Arthur Gardiner Butler

with an introduction by Jackson Chambers

This work contains material that was originally published in 1907.

This publication is within the Public Domain.

*This edition is reprinted for educational purposes
and in accordance with all applicable Federal Laws.*

Introduction Copyright 2018 by Jackson Chambers

Self Reliance Books

Get more historic titles on animal and stock breeding, gardening and old fashioned skills by visiting us at:

http://selfreliancebooks.blogspot.com/

Introduction

I am pleased to present this third title in the "Cage Birds" series.

The work is in the Public Domain and is re-printed here in accordance with Federal Laws.

As with all reprinted books of this age that are intended to perfectly reproduce the original edition, considerable pains and effort had to be undertaken to correct fading and sometimes outright damage to existing proofs of this title. At times, this task is quite monumental, requiring an almost total "rebuilding" of some pages from digital proofs of multiple copies. Despite this, imperfections still sometimes exist in the final proof and may detract from the visual appearance of the text.

I hope you enjoy reading this book as much as I enjoyed making it available to readers again.

Jackson Chambers

CONTENTS.

PUBLISHER'S NOTE.

Readers of this work who may experience any difficulty with their birds are advised to consult the "Answers to Queries" columns of **Canary and Cage-Bird Life,** *published every Friday, price One Penny. Aviculturists will find in its weekly numbers much of interest, in the shape of articles by leading authorities, and illustrations by the best artists.*

INTRODUCTION.

Amongst technical ornithologists it has been a custom, much to be deplored, to describe all birds in which the sexes do not exhibit marked differences in colour of plumage, or well-defined external ornamentation, as follows :—" Female similar to male ; " but happily, in the recent work done in the United States, where the most careful measurements of every part of each individual of a species are being recorded, and where considerable trouble is taken to ascertain the sex of preserved skins, the more or less constant differences which presumably exist between the sexes of all birds are beginning to be made apparent.

To anyone who has for many years had his eyes trained to appreciate slight differences of outline and colouring, characters unnoticed by the more superficial observer are at once evident ; he looks at his birds almost with the microscopic recognition of features observable by themselves ; and thus is in a position not only to distinguish the sexes, but to point out to others the peculiarities by which they may be identified : that this cannot be done in every case, is only evidence that even the trained eyesight of man is not perfect enough to discover at once all those details which one would suppose must be patent to a bird when seeking its mate ; nevertheless it is conceivable that no external distinctions may exist, in a few rare cases, and that in such instances a difference of scent, or tone of voice, may be the guide.

The object of the present work is to enable owners of birds to decide to what sex they belong, and I hope that the labour which I have expended upon the study of external sexual differences, embodied in the ensuing chapters, will prove useful not only to the student of birds in captivity, but of cabinet specimens : primarily, I naturally offer it as a sort of *vade mecum* for the use of aviculturists, and should it only be of assistance to them, I shall feel amply repaid for the time and trouble which I have expended in its production.

It now only remains to thank those who have encouraged me in my work, among whom I must especially mention my former Museum colleagues, Dr R. Bowdler Sharpe and Mr W. R. Ogilvie Grant, as well as their assistants, Mr Charles Chubb and Mr James Wells, who have given me every facility in examining the unrivalled collection of bird-skins under their charge.

The following works have been referred to in these articles :—

The Avicultural Magazine, 1st and 2nd series, 8vo.
Butler, A. G., *British Birds with their Nests and Eggs*, vols. i.-iii., 4to.
        Hints on Cage-Birds, 8vo.
        Foreign Bird-Keeping, 4to.
        Foreign Finches in Captivity, 1st edition, 4to.
Congress of Arts and Sciences, Universal Exposition, St Louis, 1904, vol. v.
Gadow, Hans, *Catalogue of Birds in British Museum*, vol. viii., 8vo.
Gould, John, *Handbook of Birds of Australia*, vols. i. and ii., 8vo.
Jerdon, T. C., *Birds of India*, vols. ii. and iii., 8vo.
List of Animals in the Gardens of the Zoological Society, 9th edition, 1896, 8vo.
Proceedings of the United States National Museum. vol. xxviii.
Ridgway, Robert, *Birds of North and Middle America* vols. i. and ii.
Russ, Karl, *Die Fremdländischen Stubenvögel*, vols. i. and ii., 8vo.
        Handbuch für Vogelliebhaber, 8vo.
Salvadori, T., *Catalogue of Birds in the British Museum*, vols. xx. and xxi., 8vo.
Saunders, Howard, *A Manual of British Birds*, 8vo.
Sclater, P. L., *Catalogue of Birds in the British Museum*, vol. xi., 8vo.
Sclater and Hudson, *Birds of the Argentine Republic*, vol. i., 8vo.
Seth-Smith, David, *Parrakeets*, 8vo.
Sharpe, R. B., *Catalogue of Birds in the British Museum*, vols. vi., xii. and xiii., 8vo.
Shelley, G. E., *Birds of Africa*, vols. iii.-v., 8vo.
Stark and Sclater, *Birds of South Africa*, vols. i.-iii., 4to.
Whitaker, J. I. S., *Birds of Tunisia*, vol. i., 8vo.
The Zoologist for 1900, 8vo

Many other works have been consulted, but without yielding any information of the slightest use to me, so that it is not worth while to note them here.

A. G. Butler.

July 1907.

HOW TO SEX CAGE BIRDS.

—◆◆◆—

BRITISH THRUSH-LIKE BIRDS.

THE characters which distinguish the male and female in cage-birds have been a favourite study of mine for many years, but my first paper on this subject was published in 1897, and entitled, "On Sexual Distinctions in Finches which are Similarly Coloured in Both Sexes" (*Avicultural Magazine*, vol. iii. pp. 104-106). Since that date I have published a fair number of articles dealing with the same subject, both in *The Avicultural Magazine* and *The Zoologist*, as well as a chapter in my little handbook *Hints on Cage-Birds*.

I am so frequently asked how the sexes of various birds can be distinguished, that it has· seemed good to the Editor of *The Feathered World* and *Canary and Cage-Bird Life* to ask me to prepare the present work for publication, to enable bird-lovers to distinguish the sex of all the better known British cage-birds and of the more familiar foreigners which they may chance to own ; and in order that there may be no undue preference given to the· study of our native birds, it is proposed that these articles should deal, so far as possible, alternately with British and foreign species. I shall begin with

The Thrushes (*Turdidæ*).

In its widest sense the family of Thrushes includes the typical Thrush-like birds, the Warblers and the Accentors, all of which have the young spotted on the breast ; in its more restricted sense it is represented by the Throstles, Blackbirds or Ouzels, Robins, Nightingales, and Chat-like birds. Why the latter are, in works on British birds, placed between the closely related Blackbirds and Robins I could never understand ; and I do not intend to blindly follow that plan here.

An examination of the sexes in the true Thrushes shows that the cocks, although slimmer than their hens, are larger birds—that is to say they are longer, owing to the greater length of their tails and of their more slender bills. Their general outline is not so stout and "stocky" (as the florists say) as that of their hens, so that they not only are, but appear, more alert.

THE MISSEL THRUSH (*Turdus viscivorus*).

Apart from the differences given above, I know of no constant characters by which males can be distinguished from females. It is possible that in this and the other Throstles it may be practicable to find some slight colour differences in birds from the same nest. I believe I noted such indications in a pair which I hand-reared in 1886, though (after so long a lapse of time) I cannot pretend to speak with certainty; but one thing I did observe, which would upset all attempts to base a sexual distinction upon colouring, that age gradually modified deep buff on the breast to buffish-white, so that if we were to rely upon depth of colour we might easily associate as sexes two cocks of different ages.

THE FIELDFARE (*Turdus pilaris*).

Beyond the difference in form, with length and slenderness of bill, I know of no character by which the sexes of this bird can be recognised; but I have not had the chance of examining many living examplés, and have personally only kept one cock-bird as a pet.

THE SONG-THRUSH (*Turdus musicus*).

Some bird-owners have stated that it is possible to tell the sexes of this species by the number and size of the spots on the breast, as well as by the tint. I have at various times caught and kept a good many examples of this Throstle, but I never could convince myself that these differences had anything to do with sex; they appeared to me to be either individual or due to age. If you catch your own birds, you will generally find that a cock, when first handled, utters a sort of trill or rattling whistle, whereas a hen is frequently mute; but there may be exceptions to this rule. For certainty there can be nothing better than such fixed characters as the more slender outline of the male bird, with the narrower crown and bill.

THE REDWING (*Turdus iliacus*).

There is little, if any, colour difference in the sexes of the Redwing. In the pair which I kept for two or three years in one of my aviaries, I tried to persuade myself that the hen was not quite so brilliantly coloured as her mate, but I believe it was more fancy than fact. Apart from his rather more elegant form, I knew the cock by his charming song.

THE BLACKBIRD (*Merula merula*).

In the Blackbird, apart from its well-defined structural differences, the hen is easily recognisable by her brown colouring, with more rufous throat and breast streakily spotted with blackish. With advanced age the throat gradually becomes whitish, sometimes quite white on the chin, and the black streaking more and more defined; the outline of the gape also becomes more or less bordered with ochreous yellow. Nestling birds much resemble the hen in general appearance, but the cocks are slightly larger and more deeply coloured than the hens.

The Ring-Ouzel (*Merula torquata*).

The female is paler and browner than the male, and the belt on the throat is brownish instead of white. I have adopted the generic name *Merula* for the Ouzels or Blackbirds as a convenience, to distinguish them from the Throstles; with these we begin to see good reliable colour-differences in the sexes.

MALE BLACKBIRD.

FEMALE BLACKBIRD.

The Robin (*Erithacus rubecula*).

The actions of this bird are very similar to those of the Blackbird, and among the foreign relatives of the latter are certain Thrushes, which, from their cinnamon breasts, seem to me to link the Redbreast to the preceding larger types more closely than the Chats. As I have shown in *Hints on Cage-Birds*, p. 32, the structural differences in the Robin are similar to those of the larger Thrushes. In addition to the above, the female has the forehead, sides of face behind the bill, and the chin more smoky, and the middle of the throat of a duller and more sandy hue than in the male; thus it is easy to distinguish a cock Robin at a glance by the uniform bright cinnamon of its forehead, chin, and throat.

SEXUAL DIFFERENCES IN HEADS OF ROBINS.

THE NIGHTINGALE (*Daulias luscinia*).

The Nightingale is practically a more uniformly coloured Robin: and in Stark and Sclater's *Birds of South Africa* the Eastern Nightingale is referred to the same genus as our Redbreast. Unlike the Robin, however, there appears to be little if any colour difference in the sexes of the Nightingale, so that one must determine the male by its narrower form and more delicate, longer bill. The hen of the Eastern Nightingale is said to be larger than the cock, but I suspect it would be more correctly described as stouter.

THE RED-SPOTTED BLUETHROAT (*Cyanecula succica*).

There seems to be a difference of opinion among ornithologists as to whether this lovely little bird is more nearly related to the Robins or the Chats; some say that its actions closely resemble

AN ADULT NIGHTINGALE.
(*Photographed by Mr H. Puryer.*)

STONECHAT.

those of the Redbreast, others that they are far more Chat-like. Undoubtedly the scheme of colouring recalls that of the Wheatears, next to which I should be inclined to place it. The female is altogether duller than the male, and except in old age shows none of the blue and chestnut which characterise the cock bird; the belt across her chest is also dark brown instead of black.

The Wheatear (*Saxicola œnanthe*).

In this bird the upper parts of the male are grey, but of the female buffish-brown; the under parts of the male are pale buff, deeper (sometimes almost cinnamon) on throat and breast; in old birds, whitish with buff throat and breast; in the female the under parts are pale buffish-brown; the ear-coverts of the male are black, but of the female brown. After the autumn moult, owing to the pale buff fringes to the feathers, the male much more nearly resembles the female.

The Whinchat (*Pratincola rubetra*).

The sexes are much alike; but the female is paler throughout than the male, all the black characters of the latter being replaced by brown, and the white less pure.

The Stonechat (*Pratincola rubicola*).

In this species the female is altogether much duller in colouring than the male, being browner throughout, with reddish-brown upper tail-coverts, black-mottled throat, and all the white of the male suffused with a rufous tint.

The Redstart (*Rubicola phœnicurus*).

The hen Redstart differs remarkably from the cock, being a brown bird, without the distinctive white forehead and black mask characteristic of the male sex, or the rich chestnut of the breast and flanks; the vent and tail, though chestnut, are not so bright in colour as in the male.

The Black Redstart (*Ruticilla titys*).

The female of this showy bird is quite unlike the male, being mostly sooty-brown in colour; even the cinnamon of the upper and under tail-coverts, and the white borders to the secondaries, which it has in common with its mate, are dulled by a brown suffusion.

This completes the more typical familiar British Thrushes belonging to the subfamily *Turdinæ*. The next group of Thrush-like birds of our islands which I shall have to deal with is the subfamily *Sylviinæ*, or Warblers.

CHAPTER II.

FOREIGN THRUSH-LIKE BIRDS.

THE typical foreign Thrushes are rarely imported into this country, and of the ten or eleven species which occasionally come to hand, nearly all have found their way to public Zoological Gardens; but three or four years ago Mr E. W. Harper brought home from India a nice little consignment of Ouzels, and of the Grey-winged species he gave away several to owners of aviaries in England: of one of them I was a recipient. In their sexual characters the structural features are, as might be expected, similar to those of the European Thrushes, the males being more slender in build, with longer and narrower bills than the females.

THE GREY-WINGED OUZEL (*Merula boulboul*).

The male is black, with a whitish-edged grey patch on the wing; the female brownish-ashy, paler below, and with whitish-edged red-brown patch on the wing.

I have had to sex most of the succeeding groups of Thrush-like birds by comparison of numerous skins in the collection of the Natural History Museum; this is a far more difficult proceeding than when one has undoubted adult living examples, or skins of such as one has kept, and therefore knows to a certainty that they are adult. In young birds, even after their assumption of full plumage the bill still retains some of the character of the nestling, so that it corresponds with that sex which, when adult, retains the broader bill; however, with a good series, one can arrive at the truth. The carelessness of collectors and taxidermists sometimes complicates matters, undoubted males being occasionally labelled as females, and *vice versa*.

In the Rock-Thrushes (*Monticola*) the female is noticeably smaller than the male; but, unlike the typical forms of Thrush, the female has the more slender bill.

COMMON ROCK-THRUSH (*Monticola saxatilis*).

The female is without the bright colours of the male, to which it bears little resemblance; its upper surface being greyish-brown with darker streaking and paler mottling; the under-surface yellowish-brown, with dark bars; sides of head and throat whitish; wing-coverts and tail brownish-red.

In the Dayal-birds (*Copsychus*) the bill of the male is considerably longer and more slender than that of the female; the entire bird also is longer.

INDIAN DAYAL-BIRD (*Copsychus saularis*).

The male is practically a blue-black and white bird ; the female is slate-grey above ; with throat and breast ashy ; wings brown ; abdomen sandy brown, whitish in centre.

In the Shamas there is much less structural difference in the sexes than in the Dayal-birds, but the base of the bill seen from above is wider in the hen birds than in the cocks.

INDIAN SHAMA (*Cittocincla macrura*).

The female is a duller-coloured bird than the cock, the blue-black of the male being represented by smoky black, but that of the back more ashy ; the flights with narrower pale borders ; the white tipping to the four outer tail-feathers much restricted ; under surface distinctly paler than in the male.

In the American Blue-Bird (the Blue-Robin of the dealers) the sexes differ structurally exactly as in the true Thrushes, though the difference of size is perhaps less marked than in our Blackbird.

THE BLUE-BIRD (*Sialia sialis*).

The hen is duller and perhaps greyer than the cock, her head and bill tinged with brown.

The true Mocking-Birds (*Mimus*) are extremely difficult to sex. The bill varies so much at different ages, that without having undoubted fully adult specimens of both sexes before one it is impossible to speak positively, but it appears to be rather more slender in the male than the female.

NORTH AMERICAN MOCKING-BIRD (*Mimus polyglottus*).

The throat in adult males is certainly whiter than in the females and without any grey mottling at the sides ; in young females the whole under-surface is distinctly greyer than in male birds.

The structural differences in the **Liotriges** are very slight, and difficult to define. In *Foreign Bird-Keeping*, p. 12, I have indicated the very slight difference in form of bill which I could detect in undoubted sexes, but they are hardly marked enough to be of much use to bird-owners. The male in fully adult birds is slightly larger than the female, but the difference is barely noticeable.

THE PEKIN NIGHTINGALE (*Liothrix luteus*).

Unhappily what is true of the structural characters in this bird is equally true of the colouring. Theoretically the colouring of the male should be brighter throughout than that of the female, and I think it probable that if one could compare a hundred adults of each sex the balance of good looks would be on the side of the cock birds ; but in each sex are individuals abnormally bright or dull, so that it is possible to find male and female almost as like as two peas, so far as ordinary human eyesight can discern ; nevertheless

I think there can be no doubt that the colour difference which enables the birds to distinguish each other, consists in the sulphur yellow of the elliptical patch enclosing the eye of the male, which in the female is ashy or pale creamy whitish; however, I recommend all who want to get a cock bird to whistle the monotonous call of the hen until some bird replies with the little warbled phrase which represents the cock's reply to his mate; and let them see that they get that bird and no other; they will find it far more certain than if they selected the brightest and dullest out of five hundred or more individuals.

The Bulbuls.

These charming songsters among the Thrush-like birds are easy to sex by the form of the bill; that of the male, unlike the bill in the true Thrushes, being stronger, shorter, and with slightly more arched culmen (ridge) than in the female.

MALE AND FEMALE OF THE RED-EARED BULBUL.

THE RED-EARED BULBUL (*Otocompsa jocosa*).

In this bird the hen is slightly smaller than the cock, the back is rather of a more golden brown, and the ear-plumes are shorter.*

THE WHITE-CHEEKED BULBUL (*Otocompsa leucogenys*).

This species is so very rarely imported that I have had no opportunity of studying authenticated adults of both sexes, so cannot say if there is any sexual difference in the plumage; the sexes of all the true Bulbuls are remarkably alike in colouring.

THE CHINESE BULBUL (*Pycnonotus sinensis*).

In plumage the sexes are said not to differ. I purchased a male on June 8th, 1899; and on January 6th, 1904, my friend Mr Seth-Smith gave me another, which, from its somewhat stouter build and slightly duller colouring, we thought might be a female. Not wishing to catch my bird for comparison of the bills, I turned the second bird in with it, but they quarrelled so that I had to separate them again. As both sing equally well, there can be little question that both are cock birds.

THE PERSIAN BULBUL (*Pycnonotus leucotis*).

The sexes are stated to be alike in colour; and, as I have only had one male, I must assume that this is correct.

THE SYRIAN BULBUL (*Pycnonotus xanthopygus*).

The female is said to be similar to the male; and as this species is more frequently imported into Germany than England, I have had no opportunity of comparing undoubted adult sexes.

THE RED-VENTED BULBUL (*Pycnonotus hæmorrhous*).

No colour difference has been described in the sexes, and I have only kept the cock bird.

In the Fruit-Suckers (*Chloropsis*), which Dr Sharpe has, rightly I think, separated widely from the Bulbuls, the females are as a rule smaller than the males, and have rather more slender bills; they are always less brightly coloured, and therefore easily distinguished.

Jay-Thrushes and Laughing-Thrushes.

These birds are referred to the family *Crateropodidæ*; the former are more carnivorous than the latter and therefore are best kept in cages, unless a small aviary can be devoted to a pair for breeding purposes.

In the Jay-Thrushes (*Garrulax*) the females are slightly smaller than the males, and have shorter and more slender bills.

---

* It is said, however, that the ear-plumes vary with age, and are longer in the Nepalese bird, to which the name *O. pyrrhotis* has been given.

The Collared Jay-Thrush (*Garrulax picticollis*).

There appears to be no constant sexual difference in the plumage, so far as I could judge by an examination of skins, and I have only possessed a living male.

In *Dryonastes* the bill of the female is shorter than in the male, but I could detect no appreciable difference in width.

The Black-throated Laughing-Thrush (*Dryonastes chinensis*).

I could discover no reliable sexual difference in the plumage.

In *Trochalopterum* the female is decidedly smaller than the male, and its bill is shorter and a trifle more slender.

The Chinese Spectacle-Thrush (*Trochalopterum canorum*).

The bill of the hen is paler and the throat more brightly coloured than in the cock bird.

Other Thrush-like birds are occasionally imported, but too rarely to render it necessary to consider them in the present treatise.

Chapter III.

BRITISH WARBLERS AND ACCENTORS.

Unlike the true Thrushes, the sexes of Warblers (*Sylviinæ*) do not differ appreciably in the width of their bills, but only in the length, those of hen birds being noticeably shorter than those of cocks ; both have slender bills.   The male is slightly larger than the female.

The Greater Whitethroat (*Sylvia cinerea*).

In colouring the female can be distinguished from the male by the lack of the grey head and upper tail‑coverts, and the faint vinous tint on the breast characteristic of the male summer dress. In the winter the sexes are far more alike, so that at that season the structural differences must be relied upon.

The Lesser Whitethroat (*Sylvia curruca*).

The female is a trifle duller in colouring than the male, but its smaller size and shorter bill are its most trustworthy distinctions.

The Blackcap (*Sylvia atricapilla*).

The hen differs from the adult cock in its rufous brown cap and in its generally browner summer plumage. Young cocks nearly resemble the hens in colouring, but a stouter bill, characteristic of birds which have not been for many months out of the nest, should betray the fact that they are not adult. As all those who have hand-reared nestlings are aware, the gape of young birds is very broad, and this infantile type of bill takes a long time to modify into the far more slender adult form ; it certainly is not perfected after the completion of the first moult in the soft-billed birds, as I proved in the case of such as I hand-reared, or which were bred in my aviaries.

THE BARRED WARBLER (*Sylvia nisoria*).

Although a somewhat rare visitor to our islands, this bird has been exhibited at London shows, and therefore should be noted. The female is slightly browner than the male, and has fewer transverse bars, those which it possesses being also less defined during the summer, though not in the winter.

THE GARDEN WARBLER (*Sylvia hortensis*).

During the summer the female is slightly paler than the male, but in winter they are much alike in plumage.

THE DARTFORD WARBLER (*Sylvia undata*).

In the female the under parts are paler than in the male.

THE GOLDEN-CRESTED WREN (*Regulus cristatus*).

In this charming little Warbler the hen is less brightly coloured than the cock, the yellow crest-like streak clouded with brownish, and with narrower black borders. I have never seen the so-called crest erected, though I have carefully watched pairs of this species from time to time in my garden, and therefore I doubt the correctness of illustrations which show this bird with a true crest.

THE FIRE-CRESTED WREN (*Regulus ignicapillus*).

The female is duller in colouring than the male, and its yellow crest-patch is paler.

THE YELLOW-BROWED WARBLER (*Phylloscopus superciliosus*).

This pretty little bird appears to be on the increase as a visitor to the British Islands. I have once seen it in the autumn in my suburban garden. The plumage of the sexes is extremely similar.

THE CHIFFCHAFF (*Phylloscopus rufus*).

In this species the sexes are remarkably alike in colouring, the shorter bill of the hen being the best character for distinguishing it.

THE WILLOW-WARBLER (*Phylloscopus trochilus*).

Here again the sexes are very similar in colouring, no constant differences having been pointed out.

THE WOOD-WARBLER (*Phylloscopus sibilatrix*).

No difference of plumage has been recorded in the sexes.

The Reed-Warbler (*Acrocephalus streperus*).

The sexes are very similar in colouring.

The Marsh-Warbler (*Acrocephalus palustris*).

Here again no sexual colour difference has been recorded.

The Sedge-Warbler (*Acrocephalus phragmitis*).

The hen is slightly duller than the cock, and the rump and upper tail-coverts are less distinctly reddish.

The Grasshopper Warbler (*Locustella nævia*).

The sexes are extremely similar, and no colour differences have been noted.

Savi's Warbler (*Locustella luscinioides*).

No difference of plumage has been recorded in the sexes of this bird.

From the preceding observations it will be seen how important a structural character is for discriminating between males and females of the Warblers ; as a rule, the differences in plumage are so slight that even the best observers have failed to recognise them. Then, again, the summer and winter plumages and the colouring of adults and nestlings differ more or less markedly from one another, so that only by securing birds of the same age, and comparing them at the same time of year, would it be possible to ascertain whether any reliable difference actually existed. The best way to attain definite results would be to accumulate skins of birds which have lived over a year in captivity, the sex of which had been ascertained by careful dissection after death, the date of the bird's decease being also recorded on a label attached to it.

The Accentors.*

In my account of the Hedge Accentor in *British Birds with their Nests and Eggs*, vol. i. p. 132, I have stated that the female has the bill slightly broader than the male. Recently, after examining various Warblers at the Natural History Museum, I found that I had no time left to look up the Accentors ; I therefore wrote to Mr C. Chubb asking him if he could spare time to look into this matter for me. He replied most kindly, as follows :—

"I have compared seventeen females and twelve males of *Accentor modularis*, and have come to the conclusion that the bill of the female is slightly the longer, but the differences are so slight as to be scarcely perceptible in measurement; however, I found that the length of the bill in the female varied from 0·5 to 0·7 inch, and in the male from 0·55 to 0·65. I also measured the width of the bill at the nostrils, but could not distinguish any difference, 0·2 to 0·25 inch."

* It is probable, if we could compare expanded wings, both of the Warblers and Accentors, that they would afford more stable characters for separating the sexes than the bills : I hope this may eventually be possible.

It will, however, be apparent (from the above variations in length and width in individuals of the same species) that there must have been birds of the year in their first adult plumage, as well as older birds, in the series which Mr Chubb compared; it is this apparent variation which practically prevents a cabinet-ornithologist from seeing the value of such structural characters as we students of living birds find most useful. Fortunately, there is no necessity to worry much over the character of the bill in the adult Hedge Accentor, because the sexes are easily recognisable by their plumage.

THE HEDGE ACCENTOR (*Accentor modularis*).

The female has the smoky ash-colour of the head suffused with a buffish tinge, and streaked with blackish-brown much more than in the male; the flanks are also more distinctly streaked—in fact, the hen is seen at a glance to be generally paler and browner, and with less grey on the head than the cock.

THE ALPINE ACCENTOR (*Accentor collaris*).

Of this handsome species, which is occasionally exhibited at bird shows, the sexes are very similar, but the female is more dingy in colouring than the male. Although a rare visitor to our islands, I once caught a specimen in the young plumage, in which the white of the throat was barely perceptible, and the feathering spotted with rufous; unhappily, I did not recognise the importance of my capture until it was too late. This bird was exceptionally wild, and fairly knocked itself to pieces, then contracted a disease which still further disfigured it; when it died the skin was not worth preserving.

The Dippers (*Cinclidæ*) can hardly be regarded as cage-birds, being difficult to keep even in aviaries, so that they need not be considered here.

In order to avoid getting the classification of the groups too much confused, it is necessary to continue here with the British forms.

CHAPTER IV.

TITS, WAGTAILS, FLYCATCHERS, SWALLOWS, ETC.

THE Titmice (*Parinæ*), with which the Bearded Reedling has been improperly associated, do not structurally show very marked external sexual characteristics; the cocks are, I should judge, slightly larger than the hens, and have rather more powerful bills, but the difference in the latter is not great; it is possible that better characters might be discovered in the expanded wings, but this will have to be decided by subsequent workers.

A GROUP OF BLUE TITS.

LONG-TAILED TIT.

LONG-TAILED TIT (*Acredula caudata*).

In the female the black stripe from eye to nape is broader than in the male; no other difference in the plumage has been recorded.

GREAT TIT (*Parus major*).

The female is duller in colouring than the male, the longitudinal black ventral stripe decidedly narrower.

THE COAL-TIT (*Parus ater*).

The female is not so brightly coloured as the male, and the white patches on face and nape are suffused with yellow.

THE MARSH-TIT (*Parus palustris*).

The sexes scarcely differ in plumage; perhaps the black cap is slightly duller, but even this may be a matter of age rather than sex.

THE BLUE-TIT (*Parus cœruleus*).

The hen is duller in colouring than the cock, with somewhat ashy cheeks, and the yellow of the under parts suffused with olive-greenish.

THE CRESTED TIT (*Parus cristatus*).

The crest is shorter and the black throat-patch more restricted in the hen bird.

The Nuthatches (*Sittidæ*).

In these birds the bill of the adult hen is longer and more slender than that of the cock; the lower margin of the bill is straighter, not bent abruptly upwards from the middle as in the cock bird.

THE GREAT TIT.

The Common Nuthatch
(*Sitta cæsia*).

The colouring is very similar in the sexes, but the female is a trifle duller than the male, with the chestnut on the flanks less pronounced.

The Wrens (*Troglodytidæ*).

When adult, the hen is rather smaller than the cock; the bill varies enormously with age, and seems to afford no constant character for distinguishing the sexes.

The Common Wren
(*Troglodytes parvulus*).

THE MARSH-TIT.

The female is rather duller than the male, and has paler legs, but there does not appear to be any other reliable difference in plumage or colour.

THE COAL-TIT.

The Creepers (*Certhiidæ*).

So far as I could judge by a careful comparison of the large series in the Natural History Museum, the fully adult female is a trifle smaller than the adult male; the bills vary so much with age that it is difficult to form a decided opinion as to whether they present any sexual differences; I do not think they do.

The Tree - Creeper
(*Certhia familiaris*).

The sexes are generally briefly described as "similar," but, from my comparison of numerous examples, I came to the conclusion that the streaking of the upper parts was darker and more regular in female than in male birds.

The Wagtails (*Motacillidæ*).

The females have rather smaller bills, with a slightly broader base than the males; but the differences are not very strongly pronounced, and require careful comparison to reveal them.

THE PIED WAGTAIL (*Motacilla lugubris*).

The female is greyer on the upper surface than the male.

THE WHITE WAGTAIL (*Motacilla alba*).

The female is rather duller than the male, and generally has the throat nearly white; but sometimes with darkish brown feathers, especially at the sides.

THE COMMON WREN.

THE GREY WAGTAIL (*Motacilla melanope*).

The female is rather smaller than the male, and has a shorter tail; her plumage is duller, and shows little or no black on the throat.

THE BLUE-HEADED WAGTAIL (*Motacilla flava*).

The female is duller in plumage than the male, and the head is more olive-tinted.

THE YELLOW WAGTAIL (*Motacilla raii*).

The female is browner on the upper parts and paler on the under parts than the male; the eyebrow streak is also whiter.

The Pipits (*Anthus*).

In this group of *Motacillidæ* the adult bill of the female is a trifle heavier, especially towards the tip, than in the male; in the latter sex it is more finely tapered off.

THE TREE-PIPIT (*Anthus trivialis*).

The female is a trifle smaller than the male, and her breast-spots are not so pronounced.

THE MEADOW-PIPIT (*Anthus pratensis*).

The female, as in most if not all of the species in this genus, is probably rather smaller than the male; her under parts are less boldly streaked.

THE TAWNY-PIPIT (*Anthus campestris*).

The smaller size of the hen is the only recorded distinction in this summer visitor.

RICHARD'S PIPIT (*Anthus richardi*).

This autumn visitor to the British Islands also differs sexually in the inferior size of the female; no colour difference has been indicated.

THE ROCK-PIPIT (*Anthus obscurus*).

No difference of plumage has been described, but it is probable that the female is slightly smaller than the male.

The Orioles (*Oriolidæ*).

In these handsome birds the bills are very similar in the sexes, and it needed a good deal of careful comparison to convince me that in adult females they actually were slightly narrower and longer than in adult males; I fear the difference is too slight to be valuable. Fortunately, there are well-marked colour differences in the sexes, which should enable anyone to distinguish male from female.

THE GOLDEN ORIOLE (*Oriolus galbula*).

The female is much duller than the adult male, altogether greener, the black on the plumage replaced by dark brown; the throat, breast, and centre of belly whitish, the two former and the flanks streaked with greyish.

The Shrikes (*Laniidæ*).

Here again the sexual differences in the bills are very trifling. In the female the bill is very slightly narrower at the base and broader towards the tip than in the male.

THE GREAT GREY SHRIKE (*Lanius excubitor*).

The female is rather duller in colour than the male, and has the neck and breast barred with greyish-brown.

THE RED-BACKED SHRIKE (*Lanius collurio*).

The female is very unlike the male; reddish-brown above, slightly barred on the mantle; below buffish white, barred with brown, excepting in the centre; no black on the head, but a pale buff eyebrow-streak.

THE WOODCHAT SHRIKE (*Lanius pomoranus*).

The female is duller in plumage than the male, the black parts suffused with reddish.

The Waxwings (*Ampelidæ*).

After careful examination I failed to discover any appreciable difference in the bills of male and female; if any exists, the male bill is possibly a trifle heavier than that of the female, but one may look too long for a character, and perhaps imagine its existence in the end; anyhow, there is no difference worthy of consideration. The tips of the tail feathers in the female are somewhat narrower than in the male, and the wax-like terminations to the secondaries are smaller.

THE COMMON WAXWING (*Ampelis garrulus*).

The female is duller than the male, and generally without white tips to the inner webs of the primaries.

Flycatchers (*Muscicapidæ*).

The females have a rather more slender bill than the males.

THE SPOTTED FLYCATCHER (*Muscicapa grisola*).

The sexes are much alike, but the female is perhaps somewhat browner and more heavily streaked below than the male.

THE PIED FLYCATCHER (*Muscicapa atricapilla*).

The female is browner above than the male, and the white portions of the plumage are stained with buffish.

THE RED-BREASTED FLYCATCHER (*Muscicapa parva*).

In the female the rich orange-chestnut throat is replaced by buff, and the bluish-grey is absent from the head and sides of neck.

Swallows (*Hirundinidæ*).

The females are rather smaller than the males, but I can find no constant difference in the bills.

THE CHIMNEY SWALLOW (*Hirundo rustica*).

The female has the outer tapering tail-feathers shorter than in the male; the colouring very slightly duller, the under parts generally whiter, and the breast-belt narrower.

THE HOUSE-MARTIN (*Chelidon urbica*).

No colour difference in the sexes has been noted.

THE SAND-MARTIN (*Cotile riparia*).

The female has a narrower belt across the breast than the male.

CHAPTER V.

WHITE-EYES, SUGAR-BIRDS, AND TANAGERS
(Family *Zosteropidæ*).

White-Eyes or Spectacle-Birds (*Zosterops*).

The bill of the female appears to me to be noticeably longer and with slightly less arched culmen (ridge) than that of the male. The two species most frequently imported are :—

THE GREY-BACKED SPECTACLE-BIRD (*Zosterops dorsalis*).

The plumage of the sexes is said not to differ, but I suspect that a careful examination will prove the cock to be brighter in colouring than the hen.

THE CHINESE SPECTACLE-BIRD (*Zosterops simplex*).

No difference of plumage is recorded ; but I easily recognised the male of my own pair by the brighter yellow of the under surface. Of course, this may vary in individuals, but I should expect a brightly-coloured bird to be a cock.

Sugar-Birds (*Cærebidæ*).

In the genus *Cæreba*, the bill viewed in profile is a little broader in the female than in the male, but I can discover no other difference.

YELLOW-WINGED SUGAR-BIRD (*Cæreba cyanea*).

The sexes are entirely different, the male being of a delicious ultramarine blue, the crown pale blue, with the lores, throat, wings, tail, and under wing-coverts intense velvety black. The female is dark green above, pale yellowish streaked with green below ; the lores and throat reddish ; the bill blackish, the feet brown.

In the genus *Dacnis* the cock is larger than the hen, and his bill is distinctly longer.

BLUE SUGAR-BIRD (*Dacnis cayana*).

Here, again, the adult sexes are quite dissimilar ; the male blue and black, the female emerald green with pale pearly lavender throat and bluish crown.

Tanagers (*Tanagridæ*).

These birds, although they vary greatly in character and colouring, are all characterised by the possession of a well-defined terminal tooth to the upper mandible, to enable them easily to pierce the skin or rind of soft fruits.   It is true that the Chaffinches have an almost equally prominent tooth, but as all the *Fringillidæ* possess a remicle (*i.e.*, a bastard primary shorter than its coverts), I do not think the length of the primary-coverts in certain genera of Tanagers is a sufficient reason for transferring them to the true Finches, as has been done by Professor Ridgway.

In most genera of Tanagers, the beak of the hen is more powerful than that of the cock, and in many species it is longer in the hen ; but these characters do not hold for all the genera or species, so that it is necessary to specify the character of the beak in each species.

SUPERB TANAGER.
(*Photograph by C. Kearton.*)

ALL-GREEN TANAGER (*Chlorophonia viridis*).

The beak of the female, when seen in profile, is narrower than in the male ; it is also a duller bird, with the blue of the upper parts confined to the back of the neck and the rump.   Why it is called "all-green" I cannot imagine.

THE VIOLET TANAGER (*Euphonia violacea*).

In the female the beak is broader and longer than in the male ; in colouring the sexes are wholly dissimilar ; the male blue and saffron-yellow, the female olive-green, more yellowish on the under parts.

The other species of *Euphonia* are rarely imported, and need not be noticed in this article. The same is true of *Hypophœa chalybea*, the Lead-coloured Tanager. In the genus *Tanagrella* the beak of the female is longer, more slender, and tapers more gradually than in the male.

RED-BELLIED TANAGER (*Tanagrella velia*).

The female, in addition to its different form of beak, is not quite so brightly coloured as the male.

BLUE AND BLACK TANAGER (*Tanagrella cyanomelœna*).

The female resembles the male in colouring, so that the different form of beak is important.

BLACK-BACKED TANAGER (*Pipridea melanonota*).

The female differs greatly from the male, being dark brown above with a tinge of blue on head and rump, instead of being violaceous blue with blackish mantle, black wings and tail edged with blue; black forehead, lores, and sides of head, and clear ochreous under parts.

In the genus *Calliste* the beak does not differ uniformly in all the species. *C. festiva* and one or two others are rarely imported.

THE SUPERB TANAGER (*Calliste fastuosa*).

The beak of the male is broader and more regularly tapered, when viewed from above, than that of the female; the latter sex has all the metallic green on head, neck, mantle, and wings of a

MALE AND FEMALE SUPERB TANAGER.

bluer shade than in the male; there is also more black shown on the mantle, owing to the narrower green borders to the feathers. The lower back and rump in old hens never attains to the deep orange cadmium of male birds, but when the cock is younger than the hen, this character fails to separate the sexes. In the allied Paradise Tanager (*Calliste tatao*) the female is smaller than the male, is less golden on the head, has the scarlet on the back more restricted, and in fully adult birds the blue on the throat duller and more restricted. Oddly enough, another relative, the Scarlet-backed Tanager (*Calliste yeni*), not only has a hen with a beak broader and longer than that of her mate, but in her young plumage, at any rate, has no scarlet on the back, but an orange patch on the rump.

THREE-COLOURED TANAGER (*Calliste tricolor*).

The female is smaller than the male, the beak very slightly broader and less gradually tapered; the green of the head less blue and more diffused; the black of the plumage dusky, not velvety blue-black, restricted, ill-defined on the throat; the orange on rump much restricted, diffused, and with dusky mottling; under parts altogether yellower and mottled with lilacine greyish.

LAVENDER-AND-BLACK TANAGER (*Calliste braziliensis*).

The name Blue-and-Black Tanager is applied by the Zoological Society to two utterly different species, which is absurd; and the present Tanager is not blue, but lavender, so that it has been necessary to rename it. The beak of the female is longer and broader at base than that of the male, and the lavender on the crown is mottled with black.

BLACK-SHOULDERED TANAGER (*Calliste melanonota*).

In the sexes of this species the beak differs very slightly; if anything, it is a trifle broader and longer in the male. The female is altogether duller in plumage; the back dull bronzy green, with dusky margins to the feathers; the rump much yellower and brighter; below it is much paler than in the male, bluish ashy on throat; centre of abdomen pale yellow streaked with greyish-lavender, but shading into yellowish-green on the flanks; under tail-coverts much more yellow than in the male.

SILVER-BLUE TANAGER (*Tanagra cana*).

The beak of the female is broader at base than that of the male, but of about the same length; the plumage is generally rather greyer.

SAYACA TANAGER (*Tanagra sayaca*).

The beak of the female is a trifle shorter, but otherwise similar to that of the male; the plumage above is rather darker, and the abdomen perhaps greener than in the male.

BLUE-SHOULDERED TANAGER (*Tanagra cyanoptera*).

The beak of the female is slightly broader at base; her plumage is also a little duller and greyer than that of the male.

PALM TANAGER (*Tanagra palmarum*).

The female has a broader and longer beak than her mate; her wings and tail are not of so dark a brown, and the pale belt on her wing is broader and more diffused.

ARCHBISHOP TANAGER (*Tanagra ornata*).

The beak of the female is broader at base, but shorter than that of the male. The colouring is altogether less vivid, with much less blue on throat and breast.

STRIATED TANAGER (*Tanagra bonariensis*).

The beak of the female is much broader but shorter than in the male. In plumage she is quite unlike it, being greyish-brown, paler on under parts; the rump and throat tinged with yellowish-olive.

WHITE-CAPPED TANAGER (*Stephanophorus leucocephalus*).

The beak of the female is a little longer and is broader towards the point than that of the male. In plumage she is altogether duller, washed above with smoke-grey, the scarlet on the crown and the lilacine white patch much restricted; under parts smoky-grey, slightly bluish on the breast.

BLACK TANAGER (*Tachyphonus melaleucus*).

The beak of the female is broader at base, but distinctly shorter than that of the male; in plumage she is utterly dissimilar, being of a cinnamon-brown colour, rather paler below.

The CROWNED TANAGER is rarely imported.

THE SUMMER TANAGER (*Pyranga æstiva*).

Not often imported into this country, but more frequently, I believe, into Germany. It is a very common North American species. The beak of the female is very slightly shorter than that of the male, but of about the same width. Whereas his prevailing colour is rosy scarlet, hers is yellowish-olive.

The SAIRA TANAGER is very rarely imported.

THE SCARLET TANAGER (*Rhamphocœlus brasilius*)

The difference in the beaks of male and female is very great, that of the male being much smaller and shorter. The female shows none of the bright carmine of the male, but is brown, with rosy reddish rump and abdomen.

MAGPIE TANAGER (*Cissopis liveriana*).

For want of authentically labelled hens, I have been unable to indicate any difference in the sexes of this species.

BLACK-HEADED TANAGER (*Schistochlamys atra*).

The beak of the female is broader in the middle, less gradually tapered, and with shorter terminal tooth than that of the male. In plumage the sexes are very similar.

ORANGE-BILLED TANAGER (*Saltator aurantiirostris*).

In the female the beak is broader from base to middle than in the male. She is a little duller in colour; the black collar uniting the stripes at sides of throat is wanting; her eyebrow streak remains permanently fulvous, and I believe the beak never becomes orange ochreous as in the male.

The ALLIED SALTATOR is rarely imported.

FASCIATED TANAGER (*Diucopis fasciata*).

The beak of the female is much wider from base to middle than in the male. I can discover no difference of plumage in the sexes.

FULIGINOUS TANAGER (*Pitylus fuliginosus*).

I am unable to ascertain anything definite about the sexes of this species for want of authentically labelled males. Dr Sclater says that the female is "scarcely darker on the throat and breast, and not quite so bright."

CHAPTER VI.

TRUE FINCHES (*Fringillidæ*).

I SHALL begin with the foreign species of the subfamily *Fringillinæ*.

Chaffinches (*Fringilla*).

These are the most typical of the Fringilline Finches, and it is always a puzzle to me how it ever came to pass that bird-catchers and small dealers have always regarded the Goldfinch as typical. The sexes of the Chaffinches, apart from their distinctive colouring, can readily be recognised by the form of the beak; that of the cock seen from above being much more bell-shaped than that of the hen. I believe that this character, and the generally greater length or strength of wing in cock birds, will be found to hold good for the whole of the true Finches, including the Grosbeaks and Buntings.

The Blue Chaffinch (*Fringilla teydea*).

The female differs from the male in being olive-brown instead of blue, with olive margins to the wing-coverts and quills, excepting

SEXUAL DIFFERENCES IN THE MADEIRAN CHAFFINCH.

that the edge of the primaries is greyish-white and the greater coverts are whitish at the ends; upper tail-coverts ashy, tail-feathers dusky with ashy edges; sides of face and under surface pale ash-coloured, under tail-coverts whitish; lores ashy whitish.

The Madeira Chaffinch (*Fringilla maderensis*).

Differs greatly in the sexes, the female above being dark ashy olive, brighter greenish-yellow on the lower back and rump; head duller than the back; the white belt across the median coverts narrower; sides of face and ear-coverts dull ashy brown; throat fulvous whitish; breast and sides of body ashy brown; abdomen and under tail-coverts white, with dusky bases to the feathers.

Rock-Sparrows (*Petronia*).

THE LESSER ROCK-SPARROW (*Petronia dentata*).

No characters for distinguishing the sexes have been recorded; but doubtless the form of the beak will serve in this as in other finches.

WHITE-THROATED ROCK-SPARROW (*Petronia albigularis*).

This species was confounded with the preceding as the young plumage, but I conclusively proved that both were adult; no sexual difference has been recorded.

True Sparrows (*Passer*).

THE CAPE-SPARROW (*Passer arcuatus*).

The "adult female differs from the male in the dark parts of the head and the throat being ashy grey, and the broad white incomplete eyebrow being separated from the white on the sides of the neck by a band of ashy grey behind the ear-coverts" (Shelley, *Birds of Africa*, vol. iii. p. 248).

THE GREY-HEADED SPARROW (*Passer diffusus*).

No sexual distinction is recorded; but there can be no doubt that the beak of the male is stronger and the wings longer in proportion in this sex than in the female.

THE YELLOW SPARROW (*Passer luteus*).

In the female the forehead, crown, back of neck, back, scapulars, and least series of wing-coverts are pale brown; under parts buff, shaded with brown on the sides of the head, neck, and body. The entire bird is smaller, but the wing is said to be of the same length; it is therefore probable that it is comparatively weaker, less adapted for powerful flight, than that of the male; the tail is shorter.

THE GOLDEN SPARROW (*Passer euchlorus*).

The female differs in having the upper parts pale brown where they are yellow in the male; mantle with a few obscure dark streaks; under parts and sides of head buff, slightly browner on the ear-coverts, and with a faint tinge of yellow on the throat; under wing-coverts buff. As with the preceding species, the entire bird is said to be smaller, but the wing of the same length.

Saffron Finches (*Sycalis*).

THE COMMON SAFFRON FINCH (*Sycalis flaveola*).

The female when fully adult is greener than the male; paler yellow below, and without the fiery orange on the forehead which characterises fully adult cock birds; it, however, takes two or three years for this bird to attain its full plumage. When younger the female is greyer than the male, and shows more green and less pure yellow in its plumage.

PELZELN'S SAFFRON FINCH (*Sycalis pelzelni*).

"Female dull brownish-grey mottled with blackish above; under surface whitish-grey, striped with dusky brown on the breast; wing and tail feathers edged with yellow" (Sclater and Hudson, *Birds of the Argentine Republic*, vol. i. p. 66). It is therefore evident that whereas the male is largely yellowish-olive, the female is largely brownish. When crossed with the common Saffron Finch the mules are perfectly fertile, and when paired successively with *S. flaveola* they gradually lose their distinctive characters.

THE YELLOWISH FINCH (*Sycalis arvensis*).

The sexes are much alike, but the female is rather duller and browner than the male.

The Serins or Canaries (*Serinus*).

THE CAPE CANARY (*Serinus canicollis*).

The adult female is "duller in colour than the male, and browner on the back, where there are distinct evidences of dusky streaks. The yellow colouring of both upper and under surfaces not so brilliant as in the male, the ashy colour of the hind neck somewhat washed with brown; the crown paler yellow than in the male, and streaked with dusky" (Sharpe, *Catalogue of Birds*, vol. xii. p. 351). The female is also distinctly smaller and has shorter wings than the male.

THE SULPHUR SEED-EATER (*Serinus sulphuratus*).

The adult female "only differs from the male in being slightly less brilliant, with the yellow stripe along the sides of the face more obscure" (Sharpe, *t. c.*, p. 353). It is, however, distinctly smaller, and has shorter wings.

ST HELENA SEED-EATER (*Serinus flaviventris*).*

The female is altogether paler, greener, and more heavily streaked with blackish than the male; eyebrow ashy whitish; the under parts ashy whitish instead of yellow; the throat, breast, and flanks streaked with dusky brown.

THE GREEN SINGING-FINCH (*Serinus butyraceus*).†

The only sexual differences mentioned by Captain Shelley are that in the female the chin is often white, and that it is slightly smaller

* Captain Shelley has recognised two species or subspecies, that figured in my *Foreign Finches* being called Marshall's Canary; but it seems probable that the differences have appeared quite recently, and are due to local conditions, so that it would be better not to disturb the name by which we know this bird.

† Captain Shelley insists upon this as the correct scientific name for the Green Singing-Finch, which he calls the "Yellow-fronted Canary."

than the male ; but in all that I have seen, the females have been invariably paler and somewhat browner above than the males.

THE YELLOW-RUMPED SEED-EATER (*Serinus angolensis*).

No sexual difference is recorded by Captain Shelley ; therefore all specimens should be compared carefully side by side, and those with different outline of beak set aside as pairs. Dr Sharpe says the female has the black on the throat broken up into spots.

THE GREY SINGING-FINCH (*Serinus leucopygius*).

The note to the preceding species applies equally to this, but I believe the females are usually more streaked on the flanks than the males.

THE WHITE-THROATED SINGING-FINCH (*Serinus albigularis*).

According to Dr Sharpe (*Catalogue of Birds*, xii. p. 360), "the female apparently only differs from the male in having some dusky spots on the throat"; but having no sexed specimens before him, he could not be certain of this distinction. Captain Shelley mentions no difference, but unquestionably the contour of the beak would be dissimilar in the sexes.

THE COMMON SERIN (*Serinus serinus*).

The female is duller in plumage than the male.

THE WILD CANARY (*Serinus canaria*).

The female is browner than the male ; the yellow on the forehead, sides of face, and under parts less bright.

THE ALARIO FINCH (*Alario alario*).*

The sexes are very dissimilar, the female having the head and centre of breast ashy spotted with blackish instead of the black characteristic of the cock; the back also is reddish-brown instead of chestnut, the inner secondaries blackish, with broad reddish-brown borders ; the under parts pale buffish-brown where they are white in the male.

The Siskins (*Chrysomitris*).

THE AMERICAN SISKIN (*Chrysomitris tristis*).

Whereas the male is yellow, the head with black cap and the wings and tail varied with black and white, the female is olive-brownish or greyish, sometimes washed with greenish ; the upper tail-coverts pale greyish or greyish-white; under parts whitish, more or less, and sometimes entirely suffused with yellowish, excepting the under tail-coverts ; the beak, which is orange-yellow tipped with black in the male, is horn-coloured in the female. In the winter the male nearly resembles the female in colour.

* *Serinus alario*, according to Shelley, who regards this as a true Canary.

Yarrell's Siskin (*Chrysomitris yarrelli*).

The female has blackish-brown instead of black wings, but with a similar yellow belt ; the tail blackish instead of black ; head without black cap ; under wing coverts and axillaries paler yellow than in the male.

The Black-headed Siskin (*Chrysomitris icterica*).

The female is greyer above than the male, rather more yellow on the rump ; the wing and tail feathers with less yellow at the base ; cheeks and under parts greyish, greener on the throat ; abdomen and under tail-coverts whitish ; the characteristic black head and bright yellow under parts of the male are therefore wanting.

The Citril Finch (*Chrysomitris citrinella*).

The female is much duller and browner above than the male ; the yellow of the forehead and under parts also duller ; it is a smaller bird.

The Totta Siskin (*Chrysomitris totta*).

The female is browner than the male, with no yellow, but blacker streaks on the head ; the throat ashy brown, washed with yellow, and thickly spotted with dark brown.

Rose-Finches (*Carpodacus*).

The Scarlet Rose-Finch (*Carpodacus erythrinus*).

In the female all the crimson and rose colour is wanting ; the general colour above being olive-brown ; the head, mantle, and back with dark centres to the feathers ; the under parts brownish, washed with buffish on the breast, the throat and under tail-coverts white ; the throat, breast, and flanks streaked with dusky brown.

The Purple Rose-Finch (*Carpodacus purpureus*).

In the female the purplish-claret colour of the male is replaced by olive or olive-greyish ; the crown, neck, and mantle streaked with dusky and whitish ; the under parts whitish with broad wedge-shaped olive streaks on the breast ; the sides of head bounded by a broad olive streak, the cheeks whitish, streaked with olive ; wings and tail dusky, with light olive, or olive-greyish edges to the feathers. In captivity the Rose-Finches moult into a plumage nearly resembling that of the hen ; therefore the beak must be studied.

Pine Grosbeaks (*Pinicola*).

The Pine Grosbeak (*Pinicola enucleator*).

In the United States, various species and subspecies are recognised, differing chiefly in size and character of beak. Those which I possessed some years ago were of the Canadian race (*P. enucleator canadensis*). The female is smaller than the male, and differs in having all the rosy wine-red of that sex replaced by coppery olive more distinctly copper-coloured on the crown, and golden coppery on the rump. Viewed from above, the beak of the hen is much narrower and less swollen at centre than that of the cock. When moulted in captivity, the male assumes much more nearly the colouring of the female, so that the different form of the beak is important.

Rosy Bullfinches (*Erythrospiza*).

THE DESERT TRUMPETER BULLFINCH (*Erythrospiza githaginea*).

The female is altogether duller and less rosy in colouring than the male, but otherwise similar in plumage.

CHAPTER VII.

BRITISH FRINGILLINÆ.

THE EUROPEAN CHAFFINCH (*Fringilla cœlebs*).

THE female is rather smaller than the male, has the crown and back buffish-brown and the under parts buffish-grey, so that there is no difficulty in distinguishing it from the male.

THE BRAMBLING (*Fringilla montifringilla*).

The female is altogether less brilliantly coloured than the male; approaching the winter-colouring of that sex, but with the black of the upper parts replaced by brown, and the bars across the wings much less prominent.

THE TREE SPARROW (*Passer montanus*).

The sexes are similar in plumage, but the female is smaller than the male, and has a shorter wing; doubtless the beak shows the same differences as in other species.

THE HOUSE SPARROW (*Passer domesticus*).

The female is altogether duller and browner than the male. The broad borders to the feathers of the mantle and back being tawny rather than chestnut; the eyebrow line and bar on the wing are less pure and distinct; the under parts browner, with no black on throat and chest. In an article which I published in *The Zoologist* in 1900, pp. 74, 75, I pointed out that comparisons of the total length in the flesh of individuals of this species, with the relative length of their wings, conclusively proved that the wing of the female was out of all proportion shorter than that of the male; where the largest hen exceeded the largest cock in size, her wing measured half an inch less in entire length.

The cabinet-naturalist, not having expanded wings to measure from, nor birds in the flesh, but only more or less distorted skins and closed wings, cannot possibly take his measurements with absolute accuracy; therefore when he gives the total length of wings in male and female of a species (even assuming that he has measured more than one example, which is not always certain), one cannot consider his dictum as final.

It is certain that if the wing of a male Passerine bird is not longer than its female, it must be so formed as to give him greater power in flight, otherwise he could not overtake his mate. For this reason it is especially important, even from a cabinet-naturalist's standpoint, that he should have expanded wings of all species before him, so that he may discover the nature of the differences which must exist.

The Linnet (*Acanthis cannabina*).

The female shows none of the crimson colouring which characterises the breeding-plumage of the male; it is also browner above, with black centres to the feathers; is much more prominently streaked below; has a broader skull and base to beak; the wings and tail show much narrower white outer margins to the feathers; the wings are also shorter, the arm to the bend of the wing shorter and less inarched; the long primary feathers more regularly graded, the primary coverts more exposed, only the second and third of the long primaries are emarginate in front (the first primary is very short, and only visible when carefully looked for); the outer tail-feathers are also much longer in proportion to the others than in the male.

The Twite (*Acanthis flavirostris*).

The female shows no rose-red on the rump as in the breeding-plumage of the male; the skull and beak, and probably the outline of the wings, differ as in the Linnet.

The Lesser Redpoll (*Acanthis rufescens*).

The female is smaller than the male; the rump and breast without the rose-red of the male in the breeding-plumage; the upper parts slightly darker, and the under parts more prominently streaked; the skull and base of beak broader.

The Mealy Redpoll (*Acanthis linaria*).

The female is smaller than the male; shows no rose-colour on the rump, throat, or breast; the upper parts are darker, the under parts more streaked; the skull and base of beak broader.

The Goldfinch (*Carduelis elegans*).

The female is smaller than the male, and altogether duller in colouring. The male, however, varies more in size than the female, but invariably has longer wings, owing to the better development of

WINGS OF GOLDFINCH, TO SHOW SEXUAL DIFFERENCES IN SIZE,
LENGTH OF PRIMARIES, AND PATTERN.

the second to fifth primaries, counting from the front (the first primary being short and only visible when sought for with a needle). The beak of the male is wider at the base, more swollen towards the middle, is slightly longer, and when viewed in profile has perhaps a straighter culmen or ridge.

With regard to plumage, the white portions are all purer, less stained with brown than in the hen. The rump is white, frequently more or less varied with buffish-sienna, whereas in the hen it is always varied with mouse-brown, and sometimes wholly of that colour. The wings are blacker in the cock; blue-black, sometimes touched with bronzy green at base, whereas in the hen they are rusty black; the wing-belt is narcissus-yellow in adult cocks, primrose-yellow in adult hens, but of the same tint in Greypates; the hinder portion of this belt is narrower in the hen, and more suffused with buff at the edges than in the cock; the crimson "blaze" or mask on the face is brighter, but varies in extent, so that the character given by catchers and others, "blaze extending to behind the eye," is not a constant male character.

I confirmed the whole of the above points in April 1903 by a careful examination of the extensive collection of skins in the Natural History Museum. To those not familiar with the sexual characters of this bird, the study of skins in any very large collection might be a trifle puzzling, inasmuch as (owing to the perfunctory manner in which collectors often have to examine their day's bag when skinning, and to the occasional carelessness of taxidermists in labelling those which they prepare for the cabinet) a palpably wrongly-sexed specimen here and there must of necessity crop up; but with the majority correctly sexed, and personal knowledge of the male and female characters, one can safely and contentedly ignore these pretenders.

I have entered thus fully into the sexual differences in the Goldfinch because amateurs find more difficulty with it than with most British birds, although its characters are so well defined.

The Siskin (*Chrysomitris spinus*).

The female is smaller than the male, with broader crown and shorter beak; she is altogether duller and greyer in colouring, with less yellow on the rump, wings, and tail, no black on crown or chin, and more streaked under parts.

The Bullfinch (*Pyrrhula europœa*).

The female is slightly duller than the male on the upper parts, and all the salmon-red of the male is replaced by soft dove-brown.

The Common Crossbill (*Loxia curvirostra*).

The rose-madder of the adult male is replaced in the female by greenish-grey washed with yellow; the rump is yellow, the under parts dull yellow streaked with brown; the throat and abdomen paler. Males moulted in captivity unfortunately assume very nearly the hen-colouring, so that a structural distinction is a necessity. The beaks fortunately differ; that of the female being longer and more slender than that of the male; in paired specimens the mandibles cross in opposite directions, but as the lower mandible is sometimes on the one side of the upper, and sometimes on the other in both sexes, it seems tolerably certain that the cock birds must select wives which differ from themselves in this peculiarity; otherwise it is inconceivable that the cock could feed his mate.

The Two-barred Crossbill (*Loxia bifasciata*).

The sexual differences in this species are similar to those in the common species.

This brings us to the end of the more typical Finches, though it is doubtful whether the so-called Grosbeaks ought to be kept dist'nct from them. The apparent affinity of the Greenfinch to the Goldfinch, and the ease with which it can be crossed with this and other typical Finches, make one sceptical as to the value of the subfamily *Coccothraustinæ*.

Chapter VIII.

THE GROSBEAKS (*Coccothraustinæ*).

The foreign Grosbeaks are numerous, but the British only two in number, so that it is not worth while to keep them separate. The females are generally smaller than the males, and have less powerful beaks.

Common Hawfinch (*Coccothraustes vulgaris*).

In the female the plumage is altogether duller and browner than that of the male, with all the white markings much less pure. The Japanese race (*C. japonica*) shows similar differences in the sexes.

Black-tailed Hawfinch (*Eophona melanura*).

In the female the head is drab-brown instead of black; the wing-coverts are ashy brown; the greater series black at the extremities; the general colouring is more drab; the tawny tints of the under parts mostly wanting.

BLACK-AND-YELLOW HAWFINCH (*Mycerobas melanoxanthus*).

Although not an uncommon Indian bird, this does not seem to be frequently imported. The female is very different from the male, above black, mottled with yellow, the wing-feathers with yellow edges; the face broadly striped alternately yellow and black, the

MR R. V. RAINE'S HAWFINCH.
(From a Photograph by Mr Wilkinson, Silloth.)

back of the cheeks and sides of neck yellow streaked with black; the under parts yellow, the breast and sides spotted with black streaks. As this does not profess to be a treatise comprising the whole of the imported cage-birds, it seems hardly worth while to consider *Pheucticus*, *Oryzoborus* or *Melopyrrha*, but a handsome bird like *Mycerobas*, which is sometimes to be purchased, seemed to me worth noting.

Brazilian Blue Grosbeak (*Guiraca cyanea*).

The sexes are entirely dissimilar. In the female the deep blue of the male, varied with brighter cobalt blue, being replaced by ochreous brown on the upper parts, more reddish on the lower back, rump, and upper tail-coverts, and by ochreous buff on the under parts.

The Common Greenfinch (*Ligurinus chloris*).

The female is much duller than the male, and browner; the feathers of the head and mantle with dark shaft-streaks; the under parts are less yellow.

Greenfinch

Chinese Greenfinch (*Ligurinus sinicus*).

The female is altogether duller and browner than the male, the ashy markings replaced by brown, the yellow on head and under parts much less pronounced; the abdomen and thighs whitish; the yellow on the wings nearly as in the male. In Japan there is a larger form (*L. Kawarahiba*), which chiefly differs in its superior size with less vivid colouring.

Lined Finch (*Spermophila lineola*).

The female above is olive-brown instead of greenish-black, with lighter upper tail-coverts; the flights and tail-feathers dusky, edged with olive-brown; lores and eyelids ochreous buff; ear-coverts pale olive-brown; cheeks and throat pale ochreous, browner towards front of neck; breast and abdomen buffish-white tinged with ochre, as also the under tail-coverts; sides of body olive-brown, thighs ochreous brown; under wing-coverts and axillaries dull whitish tinged with yellow.

BLUISH FINCH (*Spermophila cærulescens*).

The male, as is well known, is not unlike the common **White-throated Finch**, but with a black patch on the chin. The female is very dissimilar. Dr Sclater describes it as "pale olive-brown; wings and tail darker; beneath lighter, tinged with ochraceous; middle of the belly almost white" (*Birds of the Argentine Republic,* vol. i. p. 46).

WHITE-THROATED FINCH (*Spermophila albigularis*).

Unlike the male, the female is greyish-brown; the flight and tail-feathers with darker centres; the first long primaries white at the base, forming a spot in the closed wing as in the male; under parts

HEADS OF WHITE-THROATED FINCH.

white with a greyish-brown belt across the breast; beak black instead of yellow; feet browner than in the male.

LINEATED FINCH (*Spermophila lineata*).

The female is quite unlike the male; above olive-brown, yellower on the rump; feathers of wings (excepting lesser coverts) and tail-feathers dusky, edged with brownish olive; lores and feathers round eye ashy-whitish; ear-coverts pale olive-brown streaked with whitish; under parts ochraceous, browner on sides of body, centre of breast and abdomen whiter; axillaries and under wing-coverts white edged with yellow.

COLLARED FINCH (*Spermophila cucullata*).

Sexes quite unlike; the female is brown above with a slight olive tinge; the wings and tail (the lesser wing-coverts excepted) dark brown with paler borders ; lores, side of head, and under parts pale tawny buff, paler on abdomen, but darker on under tail-coverts ; under wing-coverts and axillaries buffish-white.

EULER'S FINCH (*Spermophila superciliaris*).

The female is of a darker olive above than the male ; wings crossed by two ochraceous bars (in the male they are buffish-white) ; margins of the quills redder than in the male ; eyelids and lores olive-yellow ; sides of head dull olive ; throat olive-yellow ; chest and sides of body yellowish olivaceous brown ; under tail-coverts pale brown washed with yellowish at extremities, which are otherwise whitish.

REDDISH FINCH (*Spermophila nigro-aurantia*).

Unlike the male, the female is olive-brown, the under parts yellowish-white in the centre, which deepens into ochraceous on the under tail-coverts ; the flights and tail-feathers are brown edged with olive.

PLUMBEOUS FINCH (*Spermophila plumbea*).

Burmeister did not know the female, and Dr Sharpe only notes that a female from Guiana is a much redder bird. Judging from analogy, Burmeister says it is probably of a greyish-olive colour, inclining more to yellowish on the abdomen ; but Mr F. C. Thorpe writes me that it is "uniform light brown ; paler, almost whitish, on the vent."

GUTTURAL FINCH (*Spermophila gutturalis*).

The female is dull brownish-olive instead of bright olive-green ; below it is paler and more yellow excepting on the breast, which is slightly ruddy ; the wing and tail-feathers are blackish with pale edges ; the beak is horn-grey instead of silver-grey, and the feet more flesh-coloured than in the male.

HALF-WHITE FINCH (*Spermophila hypoleuca*).

The female is olive-brownish instead of slate-grey as in the male ; the wing and tail-feathers darker brown edged with olive-grey ; under parts paler and more yellow in tint, the middle of the abdomen and under tail-coverts white ; the beak reddish-yellowish-grey ; feet pale greyish flesh-coloured.

The SPECTACLED FINCH and the BLACK-BANDED FINCH, which have appeared at the London Zoological Gardens, come from Ecuador and Mexico, and therefore are not likely to be frequently offered for sale in the living bird market.

JACARINI FINCH (*Volatinia Jacarini*).

The female is altogether browner than the male, the wings and tail darker with pale edges to the feathers, lores and feathers round eye whitish; cheeks pale brown; throat and abdomen whitish, the former with dusky mottling; throat, breast, and sides of body pale yellowish-brown streaked with dark brown; thighs and under tail-coverts similar; beak brownish horn colour.

ROSE-BREASTED GROSBEAK (*Hedymeles ludovicianus*).

The female of this handsome bird is very different from the male, being olivaceous or ochreous brown above streaked with blackish instead of the black and white of its mate; through the centre of the crown, however, it has a white streak, an eyebrow stripe and the lores are white, and the cheeks buffish-white; the wings and tail are blackish-brown, the former showing two white bands as in the male. The under parts are white, with the breast and centre of abdomen buffish (instead of the beautiful rose-red patch on the fore-neck and breast of the cock bird); the breast flanks and centre of the abdomen are streaked with brown, and the under wing-coverts and axillaries are orange instead of rose-red; the beak also is brown instead of white.

VIRGINIAN CARDINAL (*Cardinalis cardinalis*).

Instead of the bright brick red or scarlet of the cock bird, the hen is pale olive-brown, with the webs of the principal wing-feathers and the tail-feathers suffused with red, the under parts are pale buff, shading into white towards the tail; the thighs and under surface of the wings brighter red than the upper surface tints; beak similar to that of male.

In America no less than a dozen races of this bird are recognised under distinctive names, but the differences are too slight to commend themselves to the consideration of the cage-bird lover.

Dr Sharpe thought it possible that *Cardinalis* might prove to be a Bunting; but although it shows certain characteristics which seem to bring it near to *Paroaria*, I think the heavy, powerful beak of *Cardinalis* is far more suggestive of *Coccothraustes*, *Hedymeles*, and other genera of the larger Grosbeaks.

Chapter IX.

BUNTINGS (*Emberizinæ*).

The foreign Buntings are numerous, but there are only about eight British species to which we can fairly lay claim, all but two of them referable to the genus *Emberiza*. The females in this genus are generally smaller than the males, and their beaks are shorter and less powerful.

HEADS OF MALE AND FEMALE OF THE REED BUNTING.

British Buntings.

The Corn Bunting (*Emberiza miliaria*).

The female is slightly smaller than the male, and of a greyer shade.

The Yellow Bunting (*Emberiza citrinella*).

Generally speaking, the female is much less yellow than the male, with much more brown streaking on the sides of the crown; the chestnut of the upper parts is much less pronounced, excepting on the rump and upper tail-coverts, whilst the olive-brown streaking of the under parts is better defined.

Reed Bunting (*Emberiza schœniclus*).

In the female the distinctive black head and gorget are wanting, the feathers of the head being dark brown, with reddish-brown borders; the lores and an eyebrow-stripe which bounds the ear-coverts and joins the moustachial stripe pale buff; the throat white, bounded on each side by a broad blackish streak; the breast is streaked with brown; otherwise, apart from her inferior size, the hen resembles the cock.

The Cirl Bunting (*Emberiza cirlus*).

The female is much duller than the male, without the distinctive dark olive of crown and nape, blackish of sides of head, chin, and throat; yellow of eyebrow and moustachial stripes and half-collar, or greyish-olive belt across breast; it chiefly differs from that sex of the Yellow Bunting in the absence of yellow from the crown, olivaceous rump, and the less pronounced yellow of its under parts. ·

Ortolan Bunting (*Emberiza hortulana*).

The female is altogether duller and browner than the male, the head greener, and streaked with dark brown; the sides of throat, breast, and sides of abdomen also streaked.

Black-headed Bunting (*Emberiza melanocephala*).

The female is much duller than the male, and without the black cap; it is sandy brown above, with darker streaks, the rump slightly yellower; the wing-coverts and quills margined with buffish-white; the under parts dirty white, more sandy on breast and flanks, which are also narrowly streaked with brown; belly and under tail-coverts washed with yellow.

Lapland Bunting (*Calcarius lapponicus*).

The female is paler than the male above, and without the defined collar on the nape; the feathers of the crown have tawny margins, and a whitish stripe runs down the centre of the head; ear-coverts brown, partly edged with blackish; cheeks and under parts creamy white; a black line runs below the cheeks to the upper throat, where the feathers are also black, but partly concealed by broad whitish borders.

Snow Bunting (*Plectrophenax nivalis*).

In the female all the black parts of the plumage are greyer than in the male, and the feathers have pale (not white) margins; the head and neck more or less mottled with blackish.

We now come to the foreign Buntings, in considering which it is best to start with the Cardinals, as most nearly resembling the Grosbeaks.

Foreign Buntings.

THE RED-CRESTED CARDINAL (*Paroaria cucullata*).

The female closely resembles the male, but is slightly less brilliant in colour; and has a longer beak, with the culmen (ridge) less arched.

DOMINICAN CARDINAL (*Paroaria larvata*).

In the so-called Pope or Red-headed Cardinal the hen nearly resembles the cock, but the primaries have narrower white edges to the outer webs, and the beak is longer, with less arched culmen.

THE RED-CRESTED CARDINAL.

YELLOW-BILLED CARDINAL (*Paroaria capitata*).

The female is a trifle larger than the male, and is very slightly greyer on the mantle; the red of the head is also rather less brilliant; the beak is shorter and tapers more gradually; when viewed from above it has a coarser outline, not so slender towards the point, and perhaps a trifle wider at the base.

GREEN CARDINAL (*Gabernatrix cristata*).

The hen shows none of the bright yellow of the cock bird, but is altogether paler, duller, and browner; a broad eyebrow streak, a broad moustachial streak between the cheeks and the black gorget, and a narrow border to the latter, white.

The Pileated Finch (*Coryphospingus pileatus*).

The hen is altogether browner than the cock, and has a brown instead of carmine crest; it is also smaller.

Red-crested Finch (*Coryphospingus cristatus*).

The female is browner than the male, with all the crimson replaced by rosy-vinous, very pale on the ear-coverts and under parts of the body; the lores ashy whitish; crest brown instead of carmine.

Diuca Finch (*Diuca diuca*).

The female is, as usual, smaller than the male, and is "browner where the latter is grey; ear-coverts brown; cheeks, throat, breast, and abdomen white; fore-neck, chest, and sides of body pale ashy brown, inclining to reddish-brown on the flanks, and to orange on the sides of the vent" (Sharpe, *Catalogue of Birds*, vol. xii. p. 801).

Snow Bird (*Junco hiemalis*).

More ashy in the female than in the male, but tending to ashy blackish on the head and hind-neck; the penultimate tail-feather with a small brown edging to the end of the outer web, and the white on the third feather reduced to an irregular mark on the inner web.

Chingolo Song-Sparrow (*Zonotrichia pileata*).

The female is smaller than the male, and duller in colour. In the Museum Catalogue the female is said to be larger, but this is probably due to stretching of the skin; Sclater and Hudson say that it is smaller, which is far more likely.

White-eyebrowed Song-Sparrow (*Zonotrichia leucophrys*).

According to Ridgway "usually with the median crown-stripe rather narrower and greyer (than in the male), the occipital portion, and also the supra-auricular stripe distinctly grey" (*Birds of North and Middle America*, vol. i. p. 337). Doubtless, when indistinguishable in plumage from the male, the outline of the beak would suffice to distinguish it.

Indigo Finch or Bunting (*Cyanospiza cyanea*).

The female is smaller than the male, the winter plumage of which it approaches more nearly than that of the summer; it is brown above, tinged with blue on the shoulders, edges of larger feathers, and rump; below whitish, indistinctly streaked with dull buff.

Nonpareil Bunting (*Cyanospiza ciris*).

The hen is duller than the cock; above entirely olive-golden green; the under parts buffish-yellow instead of scarlet; the absence of blue from the head will always distinguish it even from those cage-moulted cocks in which the red of the under surface has been replaced by yellow; in young cocks also there is usually a trace of red on the flanks (I believe this plumage has been regarded as a winter plumage of the female, but in all the specimens which I have kept there was no change of plumage in either sex throughout the year).

Few species of foreign *Emberiza* have been imported; and those which have come into the market have chiefly been introduced singly from Japan; the two following are perhaps better known than any of the others :—

RED-BACKED BUNTING (*Emberiza rutila*).

Differs in the female by the much browner and streaked upper parts; the lower back and rump chestnut, upper tail-coverts paler, with dusky centres and ashy borders; wing-coverts dark brown, with ashy olive edges, changing to yellowish-white at the tips of the feathers; flights dark brown, with paler borders, tail-feathers dark brown with olive borders, lores, feathers round eye and a faint eyebrow streak yellowish; ear-coverts pale ashy brown, margined above with black; cheeks and throat pale ochraceous; remainder of under parts pale sulphur-yellow, with a few dusky streaks on the chest; sides of body ashy olive, streaked with blackish.

RED-HEADED BUNTING (*Emberiza luteola*).

The female is much duller than the male, with no bright orange on the crown, and hardly any yellow in the plumage. Upper parts light ashy brown streaked with blackish excepting on the lower back and rump, the latter with a sub-terminal yellowish shade; lores and feathers round eye ashy whitish; ear-coverts pale brown; cheeks and under parts sandy yellowish-grey, more yellow on under tail-coverts.

Weaving Finches (*Phoniparinæ*).

CUBA FINCH (*Phonipara canora*).

The female has the black on the face and throat replaced by chestnut; the crown dull ashy brown; under parts ashy brown, with no black on the breast; sides of neck yellow, but not forming a collar as in the male; it is also smaller than that sex.

OLIVE FINCH (*Phonipara lepida*).

The female is duller than the male; above entirely olive-green with dusky wing and tail feathers; edges of primaries yellowish; eyebrow streak pale yellowish, as also the chin; under parts light ashy; lower throat mottled with black; centre of breast and abdomen ashy whitish; under tail-coverts yellowish-white with dusky centres.

Reedlings (*Panuridæ*).

Until the natural position of this family has been finally settled, it may as well stand here as anywhere; it is certainly not related to the Tits; whereas Macgillivray, judging by an examination of its digestive organs, considered it more nearly related to the Finches. In this Stevenson agreed with him; while Howard Saunders observes: "In its digestive organs and other points of internal structure this bird shows no real affinity to the Tits; and some writers have advocated its relationship to the Finches." In *British Birds with their Nests and Eggs*, vol. i. pp. 140, 141, I have pointed out that in many respects it seems to show relationship to the Ploceine Finches. I believe that my friend Mr Frank Finn considers that some of its actions indicate affinity to the Babblers; but the matter can only be finally decided by careful dissection and comparison.

The Bearded Reedling (*Panurus biarmicus*).

The female is duller than the male, the black moustache is wanting from the sides of face and throat, nor is there any black on the under tail-coverts; the bluish-grey also is wanting from the crown, which is of a brownish-fawn colour.

Chapter X.

WEAVER-BIRDS AND WHYDAHS (*Ploceidæ*)

As there are no recognised European representatives of this family, it will be necessary to consider it and the related Starlings of the family *Icteridæ* before dealing further with British birds.* I shall follow the order proposed in my *Foreign Finches in Captivity*, where I divided the family into Waxbills, Grass-Finches, Mannikins (from the German "Mannchen," or Little Man; in England sometimes spelt Manakin, as in the Tit-like *Pipridæ*), Whydahs, and Weavers. All of these, excepting the more typical of the Weavers, belong to the Whydah-like birds (*Viduinæ*), the residue to the *Ploceinæ*. The subfamily *Estrildinæ* I adopt for convenience, though it is based upon an inconstant character.

The Waxbills, etc. (*Estrildinæ*).

I can discover practically no difference in the sexes of the Waxbills as regards the outline of the beak; it is always conical, and that of the male is hardly, if at all, broader, either at base or middle, than that of the female. There are more or less defined colour differences.

* A well-known scientific ornithologist agreed with me that the thick-billed *Icteridæ* were allied to the typical Weavers of the Old World, rather than to the Buntings; yet, oddly enough, the species of *Molothrus* have been called "Cow-Buntings.

Green Amaduvade Waxbill (*Stictospiza formosa*).

The hen is a trifle paler and duller than the cock, the throat greyer, and the black stripes across the sides of the body much greyer, less distinctly black.

Common Amaduvade (*Sporæginthus amandava*).

The female at all seasons most nearly resembles the extreme winter plumage of the male, being brown above, with darker wings, spotted with white ; a black streak enclosing the eye, and a white streak below it ; sides of face greyish ; throat pale buff, becoming browner on breast ; remainder of under parts bright ochreous, with greyish sides.

Zebra or Gold-breasted Waxbill (*Sporæginthus subflavus*).

The female is duller than the male, the yellow and orange of the under parts being much paler; it is also rather smaller.

Orange-cheeked Waxbill (*Sporæginthus melpodus*).

The female is less brightly coloured than the male, the orange cheeks being noticeably paler and duller.

Peters' Spotted Fire-Finch (*Lagonosticta niveiguttata*).

The female has the sides of the face brown instead of crimson ; the chin buffish ; the crimson of the breast altogether duller than in the male. An excellent coloured plate figuring both sexes appeared in the *Avicultural Magazine* for February 1905. At present it is rare in the bird market.

Common African Fire-Finch (*Lagonosticta senegala*).

The female has much less crimson in its plumage than the male, being dark brown above, crimson on rump and upper tail-coverts ; a small crimson spot on the lores ; under parts buffish-brown, clearer on the abdomen ; sides dotted with white ; wing brown ; tail black.

Bar-breasted Fire-Finch (*Lagonosticta rufopicta*).

Differs in the female only in having no trace of red on the wings, and fewer white markings on the breast.

Vinaceous Fire-Finch (*Lagonosticta vinacea*).

Captain Shelley has transferred this little Waxbill to the genus *Estrilda ;* neither he nor Dr Sharpe gives any character for distinguishing the sexes ; it is not common in the market. Mr Allen Silver tells me that the male has the ear-coverts, cheeks, and throat blackish, but the female pale brownish

Lavender Finch (*Lagonosticta cærulescens*).

The same initial remarks apply to this as to the preceding species ; but in the female the hinder portion of the abdomen from the thighs backwards is sooty rather than black.

CRIMSON-WINGED WAXBILL OR AURORA FINCH
(*Pytelia phœnicoptera*).

The female is much duller than the male, with the crimson colouring less prominent, especially on the margins of the mantle and flights, where it is buffish in tint; the under parts are browner, much less ashy, and far more distinctly and broadly barred with whitish. This sex is not described either by Dr Sharpe or Captain Shelley. In this, which is one of the larger Waxbills, one can distinctly see that the beak of the male is broader at base than that of the female; this is probably the case in all the Waxbills, but, owing to their small size, it is impossible to follow the difference with the naked eye.

HEAD OF MALE AND FEMALE CRIMSON-WINGED WAXBILL.

RED-FACED OR WIENER'S WAXBILL (*Pytelia afra*).

The female differs from the male "in having no red on the head; the upper parts browner, with only a slight yellow shade on the mantle; sides of head, chin, and upper throat greyish ash, the latter with obscure narrow buff bars; whitish bars on the body broader; iris light brown; bill and legs dusky" (Shelley, *Birds of Africa*, vol. iv. part 1, p. 269).

SENEGAL YELLOW-THROATED WAXBILL (*Pytelia citerior*).

"*Adult female:* Differs from the male in having no red or yellow on the head and throat; forehead ashy brown, like the crown; sides of head paler ash; chin and throat white, with narrow ashy brown bars most strongly marked on the lower half, where they are as broad as the alternate bars of white; the dark bars on the body are paler, slightly broader, and more confined to the sides of the body" (Shelley, *l. c.*, p. 271).

The broader white barring of the under parts seems to be a characteristic of females in this genus.

CRIMSON-FACED WAXBILL (*Pytelia melba*).

This bird comes near to the preceding, from the female of which its hen differs in the uniform greyish ash of the chin and throat; its legs are darker than in its own male, in addition to differences under *P. citerior*.

ROSY-RUMPED OR SUNDEVALL'S WAXBILL (*Estrilda rhodopyga*).

The sexes are said to be alike by Dr Sharpe, and Captain Shelley mentions no difference, but it is probable that the female is less brightly coloured than the male. This Waxbill, in the crimson on the wings, approaches the species of *Pytelia*.

ST HELENA WAXBILL (*Estrilda astrilda*).

The female is slightly paler than the male, and shows much less rose-red on the under parts; it is also rather smaller.

COMMON OR GREY WAXBILL (*Estrilda cinerea*).

The sexes differ much as in the preceding species.

BLUE-BREASTED WAXBILL (*Estrilda angolensis*).

Both Dr Sharpe and Captain Shelley state that both sexes of this species resemble the female of the Cordon Bleu, excepting for the purple beak. I believe, however, that it will be found on careful comparison of undoubted sexes that the male of the Blue-breasted Waxbill is much more brightly blue than the female, and perhaps more than the male of the Cordon Bleu.

CORDON BLEU OR CRIMSON-EARED WAXBILL (*Estrilda phœnicotis*).

The female is not so brightly blue as the male, and with a bare wash of it on the flanks, the crimson patch is absent from the ear-coverts. If anything, the beak appears to be a trifle wider at the base than in the male, which is unusual if constant. Captain Shelley calls this *Uræginthus bengalus*.

VIOLET-EARED WAXBILL (*Granatina granatina*).

The female is greyer above and yellower below than the male; the throat is whitish; the lilac on the face paler; no black on the throat; no blue on under tail-coverts. Captain Shelley refers the last three species to the genns *Uræginthus*.

SYDNEY WAXBILL (*Ægintha temporalis*).

No sexual difference has been indicated, but it is probable that the female is rather duller than the male. Unfortunately, I only

CORDON BLEU OR CRIMSON-EARED WAXBILL.

have one cock bird living, and skins do not satisfactorily show slight differences.

DUPRESNE'S WAXBILL (*Coccopygia dufresnei*).

The female differs from the male in having no black on the head, the sides of the head being grey like the crown, and fading into white on the chin, upper and middle throat. ·It is also rather smaller.

CHAPTER XI.

GRASS-FINCHES (*Estrildinæ*).

THE following, which have been referred to the Waxbills at various times, appear to be all true Grass-Finches :—

AUSTRALIAN FIRE-FINCH (*Neochmia phaeton*).

The female is paler than the male, greyer on the back, with greyish-brown throat and chest; the flanks paler, tinged with crimson, and more numerously spotted than in the male; the breast and abdomen buff-whitish.

RUFOUS-TAILED GRASS-FINCH (*Bathilda ruficauda*).

This bird received its Australian name of Star-Finch on account of its being mistaken for an Astrild, the spots on its body being inconspicuous, especially when compared with the succeeding species or the Diamond Sparrow. The male is more brightly coloured than the female, in which the vermilion on the face is limited to the forehead, lores, and a broad ring enclosing the eye.

PAINTED FINCH (*Emblema picta*).

The hen differs from the cock in having no scarlet on the cheeks or throat; the latter, as well as the front of the neck, black, spotted with white; body below browner, more freely spotted with white, the breast with only a tinge of scarlet; it is also slightly smaller.

Although Dr Russ included this bird among the Astrilds, he says its mode of life is similar to that of the Diamond Finch. He says the same of the next bird, which he placed among the Grass-Finches, though it had been regarded previously as a Waxbill.

Australian Fire-tailed Finch (*Zonæginthus bellus*).

No sexual difference has been pointed out; but if I were selecting a pair I should look out for narrowly and broadly barred under parts, as indicated in the illustrations of an undoubted pair in my *Foreign Finches in Captivity* (opposite p. 160 of the first edition). In *Pytelia* the dark bars across the under parts are slightly broader in the males, and the white alternate bars distinctly narrower, and I believe this is also the case with *Zonæginthus*.

The Waxbills, Grass-Finches, and Mannikins all come into Captain Shelley's subfamily *Estrildinæ*, a division of the *Ploceidæ*, based mainly upon the absence of a distinct male winter plumage. This answers very well for the African forms, with which Captain Shelley was dealing, but breaks down utterly in the case of the Indian Amaduvade Waxbill.

Parrot-Finch (*Erythrura psittacea*).

"When in *perfect condition* the cocks are brighter coloured, the red on the throat and forehead is rather more extensive, and the legs and feet are slightly darker in colour than in the hens; moreover, the cocks have an altogether bolder appearance than their wives" (D. Seth-Smith, *Avicultural Magazine*, N.S., vol. iv. p. 78). As Mr Seth-Smith has been a very successful breeder of this species, his opinion is of the more value.

Three-coloured Parrot-Finch (*Erythrura trichroa*).

Respecting this Moluccan bird, Dr Sharpe says that the adult female is "everywhere duller in colour than the male" (*Catalogue of Birds*, vol. xiii. p. 386). It is also about three-fifths of an inch shorter, which makes quite a noticeable difference in a small bird.

Pin-tailed Nonpareil (*Erythrura prasina*).

The form of the beak differs very little in the sexes, but that of the male is a trifle longer and finer at the point, giving it a slightly more bell-shaped outline when viewed from above. The female has a shorter tail, and is altogether duller; the face is less blue, and the throat shows hardly a trace; the under parts being dull ochraceous, greyish on the breast, and showing no trace of the vivid rose-red and vinaceous buff of the male. In total length the female, chiefly owing to its abbreviated tail, is an inch shorter than the male. In the *Catalogue of Birds* the female is described as having a small patch of scarlet in the centre of the breast; this must, I think, either be a very old hen commencing to assume male plumage or an immature cock bird. I have taken my characters from an undoubted adult pair, the hen of which lived in one of my flight-cages for six months and the cock for seventeen months under daily observation.

GOULDIAN FINCH (*Poephila mirabilis*).

The female in both types is smaller than the male, has a more pointed but much less powerful beak, that of the male being swollen at the sides to near the point. The colouring of the hen is altogether duller, the green of the upper parts without golden gloss, the nape and back of crown hardly showing a trace of the vivid

THE GOULDIAN FINCH.

greenish cobalt of the cock bird; the rump ashy, the upper tail-coverts much less blue; the pansy-violet of the breast replaced by dull lilac, the saffron-yellow of the abdomen by pale yellow, buffish in front and whitish at centre. In the red-faced variety the female varies much as regards the amount of crimson; frequently it is restricted to a few scattered feathers, and I have rarely seen it so well developed as in the male birds. It is probable that the same holds good for the sport of this variety with the orange or yellow face, which has only recently begun to be imported.

WHITE-EARED GRASS-FINCH (*Poephila leucotis*).

The sexes are said to be alike, and even Mr Phillipps, who persuaded the species to nest with him, was unable to point out a reliable character for distinguishing them, but there must be a difference, however slight, or the birds could not distinguish male from female.

MASKED GRASS-FINCH (*Poephila personata*).

The female is a trifle duller than the male, with less cinnamon tinting on the crown ; she is also smaller.   There is no difficulty in noticing the difference in living birds.

LONG-TAILED GRASS-FINCH (*Poephila acuticauda*).

The sexes are not easily distinguished, but the cock bird is certainly sometimes larger than the hen (not invariably smaller, as indicated in the Museum Catalogue), and has a distinctly longer tail, but these characters vary greatly; he has a bolder appearance and a slightly larger black gorget.   In my specimens the feet of the hens were of a purer ochre-yellow, but this may have been due to length of time in captivity.   My 1905 birds died soon after I bought them, and those purchased in 1906 have not bred.

PARSON-FINCH (*Poephila cincta*).

The male is a trifle larger than the female, and is purer in colouring (less grey) on both surfaces ; the head above distinctly whiter, the under parts a purer cinnamon, with heavier black gorget and snow-white lower abdomen, thighs, and under tail-coverts ; he is also more perky, and struts about with more importance than the hen.

THE DIAMOND SPARROW (*Staganopleura guttata*).

The male has a slightly broader head than the female, and his beak is deep crimson to the base, whereas that of his mate shows a band of pink at the base.

BICHENO'S FINCH (*Stictoptera bichenovii*).

The distinguishing characters given for the hen are inferior size, greater slimness, duller colouring, rather paler on the crown, and slightly narrower black bars round throat and breast ; but to this day I am never certain of these differences with the living birds before me.   I believe this and the Ringed Finch to be two of the most difficult birds to be certain of sexing correctly.   I have not kept the White-eared Grass-Finch.

RINGED FINCH (*Stictoptera annulosa*).

The only sexual difference which I have seen recorded is that in the Museum Catalogue, which indicates a shorter wing and tail for the hen.   Mrs Howard Williams, who first bred the species in England, does not explain how she distinguished the sexes ; but she probably purchased them already sexed.   I believe the posterior breast-belt is wider in the cock.   Whatever differences exist in Bicheno's Finch probably repeat themselves in this black-rumped race or nearly related species.   A strong argument for its specific distinctness is the fact that the young, according to Mrs Williams, leave the nest with the black bands round throat and breast, which are wanting in the young of *S. bichenovii*.

Zebra Finch (*Tœniopygia castanotis*).

In the female the orange cheeks, black and grey striped breast and white-spotted cinnamon sides of the male bird are wanting; it is also a rather slimmer bird than its mate, and not quite so quarrelsome, although always ready to defend its nest.

Cherry Finch (*Aidemosyne modesta*).

The hen can always be distinguished from the cock by showing less crimson on the forehead, being destitute of the black gorget, and with more uniformly grey under parts.

African Silver-bill (*Aidemosyne cantans*).

The hen is a rather smaller and more slender bird than the cock, and its outer flight-feathers are greyer.

Indian Silver-bill (*Aidemosyne malabarica*).

The hen is smaller than the cock, and less buffish in tint.

Ribbon Finch (*Amadina fasciata*).

The female is usually rather smaller than the male, and duller in colouring; she shows no pure white on cheeks, chin, or throat; the latter is whitish speckled with black; the crimson ribbon of the male bird is wanting; the under parts are dull fawn colour, with no white mottling on the chest, and the blackish bars are for the most part broken up into dots and dashes.

Red-headed Finch (*Amadina erythrocephala*).

Unlike her mate, the hen, instead of having the head and upper throat crimson, has a brown head slightly flecked with crimson, and a white throat narrowly barred.   She is distinctly smaller.

The Mannikins.

These are practically only broad-beaked Grass-Finches.   As a rule, they do not differ sexually to a very great extent, as regards plumage; but where most alike can generally be sexed with tolerable ease by the character of the head and beak.

Striated Finch (*Uroloncha striata*).

The skull of the hen is narrower than that of the cock, the beak slightly shorter and stouter, not so fine towards the tip.   The same differences apply to the three varieties of the so-called Bengalee— the supposed domesticated race.

Sharp-tailed Finch (*Uroloncha acuticauda*).

The sexes differ much as in the preceding species, with which it will interbreed.

SPICE BIRD (*Munia punctulata*).

No difference of plumage has been noted in the sexes. The female in life is doubtless a trifle smaller, although from measurement of skins the Museum Catalogue makes it half an inch longer (skins are frequently distorted by the taxidermist); the beak is of the same character as in *Uroloncha*, and doubtless differs sexually in the same manner.

A comparison of this species with *Amadina erythrocephala* will show that the Mannikins are simply duller coloured Grass-Finches; the pattern of the two is not very dissimilar.

PECTORAL FINCH (*Munia pectoralis*).

The female is rather slimmer than the male, and has the white breast regularly barred with black.

YELLOW-RUMPED FINCH (*Munia flaviprymna*).

The hen is slimmer than the cock, with slightly narrower beak; her head is less purely white; and her chest perhaps more tinted with tawny. I secured three pairs early in 1906, and shortly afterwards two more pairs were given to me.

WHITE-HEADED MANNIKIN (*Munia maja*).

The male has the beak a little more swollen towards the base than the female; she is altogether a darker bird, the head suffused with pale vinous-brown; the upper parts deeper chocolate-brown, this colour extending right up to the neck; the throat and chin hardly paler than the breast, which is dusky vinous-brown, grading into the black of abdomen.

BLACK-HEADED MANNIKIN (*Munia atricapilla*).

The female has a slightly longer and narrower beak than the male, and shows less black on the abdomen; she is also a rather smaller bird.

CHESTNUT-BREASTED FINCH (*Munia castaneithorax*).

The female is smaller than the male; the beak is weaker, finer towards tip, and paler in colour; the chestnut on the breast is said to be paler, but this character varies, the broken black belt bordering it is narrower, and the black bars on the flanks narrower; the head browner, less distinctly mottled, the back of the rump and the upper tail-coverts straw coloured, whereas in the male the rump is washed with bright cinnamon fading off into ochreous on the upper tail-coverts; the tail more ashy.

THREE-COLOURED MANNIKIN (*Munia malacca*).

The beak of the female is weaker and the whole bird smaller than in the male; her head is dead black, not glossy as in the male; and the entire colouring less bright, the flights greyer, the rump paler; the upper tail-coverts and tail-feathers duller and with less opalescent gloss.

JAVA SPARROW (*Munia (Padda) oryzivora*).

The female is a smaller and slimmer bird than the male, with narrower skull, and narrower, more regularly tapering beak, not quite so deep at the base when viewed in profile.

MAGPIE MANNIKIN (*Amauresthes fringilloides*).

The female is slightly smaller than the male, the white of the under parts less pure, washed with buffish; a smaller brown patch on the sides.

CHESTNUT-BREASTED FINCH (MALE AND FEMALE).

TWO-COLOURED MANNIKIN (*Spermestes bicolor*).

No difference between the sexes has been noted by Dr Russ, Dr Sharpe, or Captain Shelley; and I have only had one example of the species, so that I could make no comparison.

BRONZE MANNIKIN (*Spermestes cucullata*).

The sexes are much alike, but the hen is a trifle browner, the chest-patch rather more restricted and less glossy. The amount of bronzy-green which has been used as a character varies considerably in different individuals.

Dwarf or Bib Finch (*Spermestes nana*).

According to Shelley, the female "differs in being browner, with no grey or black on the head or throat ; chin and throat very pale ashy brown ; upper and under tail-coverts entirely brown" (*Birds of Africa*, vol. iv. part 1, p. 174).   This, however, is unquestionably a description of the immature plumage ; the hen may perhaps be a trifle browner and with a smaller throat-patch, but she is not destitute of one.

Chapter XII.

WHYDAH-LIKE WEAVERS (*Viduinæ*).

This group includes the true Whydahs, Fire-Weavers, Red-bills, and a few others.   They invariably differ greatly in the summer dress of the sexes, but are much more alike in winter.

The Combassou (*Hypochera ænea*).

In breeding plumage the cock is black glossed with greenish-blue ; whereas the hen presents much the colouring and general character of a small Sedge Warbler.   In winter the cock much more closely resembles the hen, but may be distinguished at once by its superior size, broader skull, paler beak more swollen from centre backwards, the much blacker streaking of the upper parts and cheeks, and the browner breast and flanks.   Owing to the black markings on the wing-coverts and the very dark flights, the pale borders to the greater coverts form a very distinct band across the wing.

Splendid Black Whydah or Long-tailed Combassou (*Vidua hypocherina*).

The female differs from the male much as in the preceding species ; the male when in winter plumage has not been described, excepting as being similar to the female, but it is sure to be a trifle larger, and probably with darker markings.

Pin-tailed Whydah (*Vidua principalis*).

Roughly speaking, the cock in breeding plumage is a black and white bird, with scarlet beak and long slender tail ; the hen is, roughly speaking, a sandy brownish bird, with black centres to the feathers of the upper parts and a scarlet beak, but short tail.   In the winter plumage the cock more nearly resembles the hen, but is distinctly larger.

Long-tailed Whydah (*Chera procne*).

The male in breeding plumage is glossy black, the lesser coverts scarlet, median coverts yellowish-white, greater coverts and flights edged with white or pale brown; feet flesh coloured. The hen has very much the character and pattern of our Corn Bunting, but has tawny-reddish lesser wing-coverts. The male in winter plumage is very similar; but, as Captain Shelley says, "differs in the wing being similar to that of the male in breeding plumage, only with the pale edges of the greater coverts and secondaries broader."

Red-collared Whydah (*Penthetria ardens*).

The male in breeding plumage is black, with a broad scarlet collar across the base of the throat; the female is smaller and somewhat like a Pipit in colouring and general pattern; above pale brown, with black centres to feathers; a well-defined yellowish-white eyebrow streak and a patch of the same colour under eye; a loral band and another behind eye black; ear-coverts buffish-brown; under parts buff, yellower on chin and upper throat; lower throat, front, and sides of chest tawny-brownish streaked with blackish. The male in winter plumage is similar to the female but larger, and with blacker centres to the feathers on the upper surface; the inner lining of the wing black instead of dusky ash, and the under tail-coverts black-centred.

PARADISE WHYDAH.

Paradise Whydah (*Steganura paradisea*).

In summer plumage the male is black, with a broad collar, continuous with a broad diffused belt crossing the breast chestnut; the abdomen white; tail very long, and lengthening with age up to $13\frac{5}{8}$ inches according to my specimens. The hen, roughly described, is an ashy brown bird with dark centres to feathers, the neck and mantle washed with buffish; crown buffish-white, black-mottled, with a broad black streak on each side; a nearly white eyebrow-stripe bounded from behind eye by a black streak; chin and throat whitish; breast ashy brown, mottled; abdomen and under tail-coverts ashy-whitish. The male in winter plumage nearly resembles the female, but the streak-like centre of crown is broader, more diffused, and distinctly sandy buff. It may be a trifle larger than the female, but the difference is less marked than in the preceding species.

YELLOW-BACKED WHYDAH (*Penthetriopsis macrura*).

The male in breeding plumage is black, with the mantle, scapulars, and lesser wing-coverts chrome-yellow; remaining wing-feathers mostly with buffish margins. The female above is ashy brown, with dark brown centres to feathers; lesser wing-coverts slightly yellowish; a pale buff eyebrow; sides of head pale brown, less mottled than the crown; under parts buff, washed with brown on sides and flanks, a few darker streaks on sides of breast. The male in winter plumage is similar, but the wings are blacker, and the lesser coverts bright yellow.

The Whydahs of the genus *Urobrachya* are rarely imported, and need not be considered here. We will therefore proceed to the Fire-Weavers.

YELLOW-SHOULDERED WEAVER (*Pyromelana capensis*).

Roughly speaking, the male in breeding plumage is a black bird with the lower half of back, least and median coverts bright yellow; scapulars, greater coverts, and flights with pale brown borders. The female is pale brown with blackish centres to the feathers; lesser and median coverts and lower half of back olivaceous-yellow; a yellowish eyebrow streak; under parts with blackish streaks, abdomen whitish. The male in winter plumage is somewhat similar but larger, and with the lesser and median coverts and lower back bright yellow as in the breeding plumage.

GOLDEN-BACKED WEAVER (*Pyromelana aurea*).

This is a rare species, and the female is unknown, but it probably differs from the male much as does the female of *P. capensis*.

NAPOLEON WEAVER (*Pyromelana afra*).

The male in breeding plumage is bright golden yellow; the front and sides of mantle greyish-olivaceous, with broad black centres to the feathers; wing and tail feathers black, with pale buffish-brown borders; sides of head, chin, and throat, back of breast, and abdomen black; centre of yellow across chest strongly stained with chestnut. The female is pale brown, the feathers of the upper parts, excepting on rump and upper tail-coverts, with mesial black streaks; wing and tail feathers blackish with pale brown borders; a broad buffish-white eyebrow streak from beak to back of ear-coverts; chin and throat white tinted with buff, excepting in the centre; breast pale brown, faintly streaked at the sides; sides of body and thighs pale brown; abdomen white; lower tail-coverts tinted with buff. The male in winter dress is similar, but slightly larger, and comparison of a series will probably show that the black streaking on the head is not so bold as in the female. The length and whiter colouring of the eyebrow readily distinguish the hen and cock in winter plumage from *P. franciscana.*

BLACK-BELLIED WEAVER (*Pyromelana nigriventris*).

The male in breeding plumage has the " forehead, crown, back, upper and under tail-coverts and sides of lower abdomen scarlet; the mantle slightly duller and more rufous; wings and tail dark brown, with narrow pale edges to the feathers; under wing-coverts and inner margins of the quills rufous-buff; chin, throat, chest, and centre of abdomen jet black" (Shelley). The female above is a good deal like that sex of *P. franciscana*, but is of a more ruddy brown and much less heavily streaked with black, excepting on the sides of the mantle; the streaking on the crown is much more slender; the eyebrow similar, being only broad and well-defined from the eye backwards; the chin, throat, abdomen, and under tail-coverts are pure white, not buffish; the pale brown belt across chest more buff in tint, much narrower, and only very slightly streaked at the sides. The male in winter plumage is said to be similar to the female, but I have never seen this phase either alive or in skin; when I do I shall expect to find some difference. The same statement is made as to *P. franciscana*, but I do not admit its correctness.

All the females of these small Fire-Weavers are a good deal alike, bearing a general resemblance to the European Sedge-Warbler in pattern and colouring. In order to emphasise the difference between the summer plumage of the cock and that of the hen, it has been necessary to describe the latter more fully both in the Whydahs and Weavers than in other groups. As regards the winter plumage of the cocks, it is generally much like the ordinary dress of the hens, but I believe that with authenticated specimens of both sexes before one it is invariably possible to differentiate them. Unfortunately, when the winter form of the male occurs in collections it is rarely sexed, so that writers have generally been contented to describe it as "similar to the female."

ORANGE WEAVER (*Pyromelana franciscana*).

In summer plumage the male has the crown, lores, ear-coverts, chest, and abdomen black; the neck, back, scapulars, upper tail-coverts, cheeks, chin, throat, under tail-coverts, and sides of abdomen fiery orange, deepening with age; the wings and tail blackish, with buffish or sandy-brown borders to the feathers; the mantle and centre of back washed with brownish, rather dulling the orange. The female is pale brown above, with broad black centres to the feathers; the eyebrow stripe is narrow in front of the eye (barely visible in life), but very broad from above eye to back of ear-coverts; the latter pale brown, with indistinct dusky mottling; chin and throat and under tail-coverts buffish-white; breast pale brown (forming a broad belt), with dusky streaks indistinct in the middle;

centre of abdomen pure white, sides coloured like the breast. Male in winter plumage much like the female, but with the black streaks on the crown much narrower and more regular, and the body below less strongly streaked; at the approach of the breeding season the borders to the feathers of the upper surface first become suffused with yellow, and those of the throat acquire well-defined yellow fringes, and so the bright colouring gradually increases from day to day. I describe from a male which died in the first stage of its change.

Grenadier Weaver (*Pyromelana orix*).

In breeding plumage the male is orange-vermilion; duller on the mantle; "scapulars with broad angular blackish centres; front two-thirds of crown, sides of head, chin, upper throat, chest, and middle of abdomen black; wings and tail dark brown, with narrow pale edges to the feathers; under wing-coverts, inner margins of the quills and the thighs rufous-buff" (Shelley). The female is pale brown with blackish centres to the feathers, the stripes on the crown regular, as in *P. nigriventris;* a broad buff eyebrow-streak; under parts white, shaded with brown on the sides and lower half of the throat, the front and sides of body; most of the feathers with dusky shaft-streaks. The male in winter, according to Shelley, is "similar to the female, but with the stripes of the throat and body more strongly marked." It is larger also.

Crimson-crowned Weaver (*Pyromelana flammiceps*).

Male in summer plumage orange-vermilion above, the mantle duller, more brownish; wings and tail black, the central tail-feathers faintly edged with buff; front of forehead, sides of face, chin and upper throat, lower breast and abdomen black, lower throat and upper breast orange-vermilion connected with the red of upper parts; sides of abdomen fawn colour; thighs and under tail-coverts rufous-buff. The hen is not unlike that sex of the Napoleon Weaver (*P. afra*), but larger, with more powerful beak; rather darker and more distinctly streaked with black above; the eyebrow streak broader, and more yellow; the ear-coverts, cheeks, chin, and centre of throat also washed with yellow, the breast slightly yellower and less distinctly streaked at the sides; the abdomen less broadly brown at the sides. The male in winter plumage is said to be similar, but with the wings blacker. It is certain to be a trifle larger.

Females of this species are often sold as Napoleon Weavers. I have had two among the few which I have bought at various times.

Red-billed Weaver (*Quelea quelea*).

This pink and cinnamon bird, with its black mask and crimson beak, is too well known to need description in its summer plumage; the female has the beak orange-ochreous, the head above smoky-grey like the mantle of the male; a white eyebrow stripe with a dark grey stripe below it; sides of face ashy whitish, a blackish

HEADS OF MALE AND FEMALE RED-BILLED WEAVERS.

streak below eye; under parts buff, ashy on chest; chin, throat, and centre of abdomen pure white. The male in winter more nearly approaches the female, but always shows a little wash of pink on the under parts, and the crimson beak would always distinguish it. Sometimes it retains its summer colouring. The form known as Russ' Weaver is not a distinct race, but simply an albinism, which often appears in old age, or in delicate young birds.

Chapter XIII.

TYPICAL WEAVERS (*Ploceinæ*).

THESE birds build nests resembling either retorts or snail-shells, the entrance being from below. These nests are either suspended between reeds or from the end twigs of branches in trees; they are more densely woven than those of the Viduine Weavers.

The genera *Spermospiza* and *Amblyospiza* have been represented at our Zoological Gardens, but are rarely imported, and therefore need not be considered here. *Textor albirostris*, which is said not to differ in the sexes, belongs to the same category. I shall therefore confine myself to the imported species of *Sitagra*, *Hyphantornis*, *Ploceus*, and *Foudia*.

YELLOWISH WEAVER (*Sitagra luteola*).

The female "differs in having no black on the plumage; upper parts mostly ashy brown, washed with yellow on the forehead, crown, back of neck, rump, and upper tail-coverts, and mottled with dark centres to the feathers of the mantle; eyebrows, sides of head, and the throat pale yellow; breast white, mottled with yellow; under tail-coverts pale yellow; bill blackish" (Shelley's *Birds of Africa,* vol. iv. part 2, p. 397).

BLACK-FRONTED WEAVER (*Hyphantornis velatus*).

Captain Shelley does not describe the female, but I believe I have a living example of this or a closely related species exhibiting the usual characteristic Sedge-Warbler type of coloration; Stark and Sclater say that it "resembles the male in winter, but the lower back, rump, and upper tail-coverts are ash-brown instead of olive-yellow" (*Birds of South Africa,* vol. i. p. 59).

RUFOUS-NECKED WEAVER (*Hyphantornis cucullatus*).

The female, according to Shelley, differs in having the "forehead, crown, and upper tail-coverts olive-yellow; back and sides of neck and the back ashy brown, with slightly darker brown centres to the feathers of the mantle"; wings and tail paler; "ear-coverts shaded with olive; eyebrow, remainder of sides of head, chin, throat, breast, thighs, and under tail-coverts pale yellow, fading into white on the abdomen and flanks. Bill brown, fading into flesh colour on the under half of the lower mandible" (*Birds of Africa,* vol. iv. part 2, p. 424).

BLACK-HEADED WEAVER (*Hyphantornis melanocephalus*).

Differs from the male in the uniform yellowish-olive of the upper parts; the paler and duller edges of the wing-feathers; the eyebrows, sides of head, chin, and throat pale yellow; breast and under tail-coverts white; flanks and thighs somewhat ashy.

The above are the three species most frequently offered for sale: of others recorded in the Zoological Society's list *H. capensis* is referred by Dr Sharpe to *Sitagra,* and by Captain Shelley to *Xanthophilus; H. personata* is, according to Shelley, the same as *Sitagra luteola; H. castaneofusca* is placed by the same author in *Cinnamopteryx, H. superciliosus* in *Pachyphantes,* and *H. brachyptera* in *Hyphanturgus.*

BAYA WEAVER (*Ploceus baya*).

The female is altogether duller than the male, showing none of the bright yellow of that sex and no trace of the black forehead, sides of head, chin, and throat; the crown is coloured like the back; there is a pale buffish eyebrow; the ear-coverts are greyish-brown; the neck, cheeks, breast, and sides are tawny-buffish; the chin, throat centre of abdomen and under tail-coverts white.

MANYAR WEAVER (*Ploceus manyar*).

Jerdon observes that "the male in winter dress is clad like the female, and has the head brown, streaked like the back, a pale yellow supercilium (eyebrow), and a small yellow spot behind the ear-coverts ; the chin and throat are whitish, and the streaks on the lower surface less developed. The bill is pale, horny, fleshy" (*Birds of India*, vol. ii. p. 349). This description, with well-developed streaking below, therefore serves for the female.

Bengal Weaver (*Ploceus bengalensis*).

As before, the bright yellow of the male is wanting in the female ; its head is uniform "dusky-brown, the feathers of the back edged with pale rufous-brown ; a pale yellow supercilium, and a spot of the same colour behind the ears ; also a narrow moustachial stripe ; throat white, yellowish in some, and usually separated from the yellow moustache by a narrow black line ; pectoral band less developed" (Jerdon, *Birds of India*, vol. ii. p. 350).

Madagascar Weaver (*Foudia madagascariensis*).

The brilliant scarlet of the male is wanting in the female, which is olive-brown, the mantle streaked with black ; the crown and nape less distinctly and narrowly streaked ; sides of head and under parts brownish-buff, whitish in centre of breast ; bill, brown instead of black

Comoro Weaver (*Foudia eminentissima*).*

The female has no red in its plumage ; the crown, rump, and upper tail-coverts are olivaceous-brown, the eyebrow and under parts ashy buff, with the flanks, thighs, and under tail-coverts browner, and a dusky band through the eye ; bill, pale brown (*vide* Shelley, *Birds of Africa*, vol. iv. part 2, p. 492).

Chapter XIV.

NEW WORLD STARLINGS (*Icteridæ*).

It used to be asserted that these birds were readily distinguishable from the Starlings of the Old World by the total want of a bastard primary. When I examined all the species which I had kept, and found a very prominent first primary in them all, this statement puzzled me not a little ; but it seems that when the first primary (now called the tenth) is shorter than its coverts, as in the *Fringillidæ, Motacillidæ, Icteridæ*, and some other families, it is now called a remicle ; and when it is longer, a bastard primary. This is a strange distinction, but is, I should imagine, a charitable arrangement for condoning the peccadilloes of venerated but departed ornithologists, some of whom asserted, and evidently believed, that these families

---

* I quite agree with Captain Shelley that this species has no claim to be regarded as the type of a distinct genus.

were entirely destitute of a first primary in any form or shape. The *Icteridæ* seem clearly to be a transitional group linking the Weavers to the true Starlings, the male of *Dolichonyx* even retaining the winter plumage of a Weaver.

The Meadow-Starlings (*Agelæinæ*).

THE BOBOLINK (*Dolichonyx oryzivorus*).

The beak of the female is rather weaker than that of the male, and not swollen at the sides when viewed from above; it is also of a reddish-brown colour. Excepting that she is smaller, the female is very similar to the male in its winter plumage, yellowish-brown above, with blackish markings; yellowish-buff below, with blackish streaks on the flanks.

THE RED-BREASTED MARSH-BIRD (*Leistes superciliaris*).

The beak of the female when viewed in profile is more slender than that of the male, and is brown. She is smaller, brownish, heavily streaked with black, the tail with black bars; the eyebrow-stripe is more buffish, not so chalky in appearance; the throat dull whitish-buff; the breast slightly mottled with reddish, and with black ticks on the shafts of the feathers; the abdomen more ashy, heavily ticked and streaked with black; under tail-coverts barred with black. The difference between the sexes is therefore very striking, the male being coloured like a Military Troupial. (See *Foreign Bird-keeping*, ii. p. 9.)

YELLOW-HEADED MARSH-BIRD (*Xanthocephalus icterocephalus*).

The beak of this species is nearly of the same form as in *Leistes*. That of the female is much smaller and rather more slender than that of the male. She is by far the smaller bird; her general colour is brown, with a dark patch at front of crown; throat brownish-white, pale orange at back; breast mottled brownish, with yellow sides; chest and abdomen brown steaked with ashy whitish; back of abdomen and vent uniform brown; under tail-coverts more buffish.

RED-SHOULDERED MEADOW-STARLING (*Agelæus phœniceus*).

The female is much smaller than the male, and has a smaller, shorter beak; her colouring is quite different, brown with conspicuous black shaft-streaks to the feathers; eyebrow-streak white; under parts pale buffish, with white abdomen, all the feathers conspicuously streaked with black; chin buff or reddish.

THE BROWN-HEADED MEADOW-STARLING (*Agelæus frontalis*).

The female has a smaller and rather weaker beak than the male; she is olivaceous-brown mottled with short blackish streaks; below paler and more finely streaked; throat sandy buff. *Agelæus ruficapillus* is a much rarer bird, the female of which is not in the British Museum; it probably nearly resembles that of *A. frontalis*.

Yellow Meadow-Starling (*Agelæus flavus*).

The female has a shorter beak than the male, and is browner, slightly streaked above; eyebrow-streak, rump, and body below yellowish; a female, probably in young plumage, is greyish below with dusky streaks.

Yellow-shouldered Marsh-Troupial (*Agelasticus thilius*).

In the female the beak is shorter and a trifle weaker than in the male; she is brown, streaked with black; with buffish eyebrow extending back to nape; under parts paler. *A. humeralis* is rarely imported. My own example is the only one I have seen in captivity, and may possibly not be typical, but it has a very striking song, quite unlike *A. thilius*.

Dark Green Maize-eater (*Pseudoleistes virescens*).

In the female the beak is longer and tapers more than in the male; her plumage above is paler and more olivaceous.

Common Cow-Bird (*Molothrus pecoris*).

The beak of the female is smaller and narrower than that of the male, and is brown; her plumage is quite different, brown mottled with black above, ashy brownish mottled blackish below; throat ashy whitish.

Silky Cow-Bird (*Molothrus bonariensis*).

The beak of the female is more slender and tapering than in the male; when viewed from above it is less full in the middle. Instead of the glossy blue-black or blue and greenish-black of the male, she is brown, paler on the under parts, and with ashy whitish throat.

Purple Cow-Bird (*Molothrus purpurascens*).

The female has a more slender, shorter, and browner beak than the male; her plumage above is pale dust-brown with dusky mottling; below considerably whiter.

Bay Cow-Bird (*Molothrus badius*).

The female apparently has a weaker and shorter beak than the male, but if all the specimens I examined are correctly sexed, it appears to vary considerably. I can discover no difference of plumage.

Chilian Meadow-Starling (*Curæus aterrimus*).

The female is smaller than the male, with a greyish-indigo gloss in place of the sooty-black of that sex; her bill is shorter and less tapering.

Orange-headed Meadow-Starling (*Amblyrhamphus holosericeus*).

The bill of the female is smaller and more slender than in the male. In plumage Dr Sclater describes her as similar, but in an example in the Museum (probably immature) the deep orange of the under parts is represented by mottling on throat and breast and the abdomen is browner.

Typical Troupials (*Sturnellinæ*).

Louisianian Troupial (*Sturnella magna*).

The female has a smaller and shorter bill than the male; above a trifle paler, so that the black markings seem more distinct; pale

HEAD OF MALE AND FEMALE MILITARY TROUPIAL.

stripes on head whiter, the black breast-belt less defined, more mottled, the white patch at sides of hind throat replaced by buffish; the yellow of under parts paler; flanks whiter, less sandy brownish in tint.

Military Troupial (*Trupialis militaris*).

The female is much smaller than the male; her bill shorter, weaker, and less curved; she is browner above, with paler edges to the feathers; more sandy brown and more regularly marked from bill backwards; tail regularly barred with black; throat buff-whitish; sides of neck, front of breast, and ear-coverts ashy, ticked with black; sides and flanks ashy olive-brown with dusky streaks; scarlet restricted to centre of breast, back of chest, and abdomen.

DE FILIPPI'S MILITARY TROUPIAL (*Trupialis defilippii*).

Very similar in both sexes to the preceding, excepting in its smaller size and black under wing-coverts; the female, however, shows less scarlet on the under parts.

Quiscalinæ.*

RICH-BLACK TROUPIAL (*Dives sumichrasti*).

The female is slightly smaller and less glossed with blue than the male; the bill, seen from above, seems a trifle narrower towards the base, but is otherwise similar.

BLACK TROUPIAL (*Quiscalus lugubris*).

The female has no violaceous gloss, but is smoky blackish, wings and tail darker, very slightly greenish glossed; below smoky brown.

CHANGEABLE TROUPIAL (*Quiscalus versicolor*).

The female is smaller than the male, and has a shorter, less tapering bill; she is much browner, and only faintly glossed with blue on head, nape, and breast.

CHOPI TROUPIAL (*Aphobus chopi*).

The female is smaller and duller than the male, and has no furrows running obliquely across the lower mandible of the bill.

The Cassiques (*Cassicinæ*).

CRESTED CASSIQUE (*Ostinops decumanus*).

The female is much smaller than the male, has a far shorter and less powerful bill; the chocolate on her lower back and rump is not so deep in colour.

MEXICAN CASSIQUE (*Cassicus melanicterus*).

The bill of the female is more slender than that of the male, is more dusky in colouring; she is smaller, greyer, and the yellow in her plumage is paler.

YELLOW CASSIQUE (*Cassicus persicus*).

The bill of the female is much smaller and weaker than in the male; she is smaller, of a duller black above and browner below; the yellow in the plumage is paler.

RED-RUMPED CASSIQUE (*Cassicus hæmorrhous*).

The bill is shorter in the hen and of a greyer colour; her general plumage is brown instead of blue-black, and the scarlet on the back is much restricted.

* I know of no distinctive English name for this group.

The Hangnests (*Icterinæ*).

BALTIMORE HANGNEST (*Icterus baltimore*).

In the female the bill is far more slender than in the male; she is much smaller, olivaceous-greyish on back; wing-feathers with pale or white edges; front of crown and upper tail-coverts yellowish-olivaceous; throat and centre of abdomen buffish; breast dull orange; sides and flanks and tail greyish-olivaceous; under tail-coverts orange-ochreous.

ORCHARD HANGNEST (*Icterus spurius*).

The bill of the female is shorter, but broader at base than in the male; above she is olive, yellower on the rump; wings ashy brown with pale borders; below she is olivaceous-yellow, the vent bright ochreous-yellow; tail olivaceous-greyish.

In most of the Hangnests, which are rarely imported, with the exception of *I. jamacaii*, the bill of the hen differs from that of the cock as in the preceding species. It seems hardly worth while to enumerate all which have appeared at various times in the Zoological Society's Gardens.

BRAZILIAN HANGNEST (*Icterus jamacaii*).

The female is slightly smaller than the male, and not quite so brightly coloured; she has a shorter bill, but is otherwise similar.

Although the American Starlings are more often than not imported singly, most of them are birds of striking appearance, and confiding in their habits. In the event, therefore, of any of my readers securing what he may suppose to be both sexes, it is important that he should be able to decide the matter with a view to breeding the species. I see no reason why this should be difficult. I have therefore indicated the sexual differences in the majority of the imported species.

CHAPTER XV.

OLD WORLD STARLINGS (*Sturnidæ*).

IN the true Starlings the bastard primary is longer than its coverts, but is not necessarily on that account longer in itself than in some of the *Icteridæ*. In 1903 I examined various genera of Starlings in the National Collection, and came to the conclusion that the sexual differences exhibited by form and length of bill in these birds were usually slight, but that they were of the same nature as in the true Thrushes. (See *Avicultural Magazine*, N.S., vol. i. p. 246.) The species of *Mainatus* are a notable exception to this rule.

Typical Starlings (*Sturnus*).

COMMON STARLING (*Sturnus vulgaris*).

The female has a shorter wing than the male, is a trifle duller, shows more sandy buff tips to the feathers, and is noticeably more spotted on the under parts.　As Dr Sharpe says, "she seems never to lose altogether the spotted character of the plumage." ·

UNSPOTTED STARLING (*Sturnus unicolor*).

The female has a shorter wing than the male, but is said to be "similar in colour."　In life I should expect to find it less glossy, of a deader black colour, with less defined bronzy-purple and greenish reflections.

Starling-like Mynahs (*Poliopsar, etc.*).

SILKY MYNAH (*Poliopsar sericeus*).

The female is probably duller than the male.　Dr Sharpe describes a female, which, however, he thinks may perhaps be immature, as follows :—" Altogether browner, rather more ashy on the rump ; the gloss on the wings and tail less distinct ; primary-coverts blackish-brown near the base, white at the ends, with a central black streak ; head whitish, ashy grey on sides of crown and hind neck ; sides of face whitish, ashy on the cheeks ; under surface of body as in the male, but light brown instead of grey " (*Catalogue of Birds*, vol. xiii. p. 44).

ANDAMAN MYNAH (*Poliopsar andamanensis*).

The wing of the female is much shorter than that of the male, but no difference of plumage is recorded.

MALABAR MYNAH (*Poliopsar malabaricus*).

The female is much paler than the male, and has yellower legs and whiter eyes.

BLYTH'S MYNAH (*Poliopsar blythii*).

The female has a shorter wing than the male, is paler and duller; more rusty above, especially on the rump and upper tail-coverts; head more ashy, sides of face and throat greyer; the rufous feathers somewhat edged with ashy whitish; culmen of bill brownish; legs tinged with olive; iris greyer.

PAGODA MYNAH (*Temenuchus pagodarum*).

The female is smaller than the male, and has a shorter crest, but no difference of plumage has been noted.

ROSE-COLOURED PASTOR (*Pastor roseus*).

The female is smaller than the male, has shorter wings, has a shorter crest, and is less brightly coloured.

COMMON MYNAH (*Acridotheres tristis*).

The female has shorter wings than the male, but no difference of plumage has been indicated.

BROWN MYNAH (*Acridotheres fuscus*).

The imported form belongs, I believe, generally to the race *A. mahrattensis*, in which the iris is bluish-grey. The female has shorter wings than the male, but appears to be similar in plumage.

CRESTED MYNAH (*Acridotheres cristatellus*).

Although the Museum Catalogue records no sexual differences, I have no doubt that the wings of the female are shorter than those of the male. As I have pointed out elsewhere, the cut illustrating the head of this species (on p. 93 of the Catalogue) is entirely incorrect in drawing, the crest of *A. cristatellus* being confined to the bill and forehead, over which it curls backwards. *A. ginginianus* seems to be rarely imported.

True Mynahs or Grackles (*Mainatus, etc.*).*

BLACK-NECKED MYNAH (*Graculipica nigricollis*).

The female is a good deal smaller than the male, but no difference of plumage has been noted.

---

* In these birds the bills of the males are stronger than those of the females.

Wattled Mynah (*Dilophus carunculatus*).

In the female the wings are shorter than in the male : she is also browner, making the white rump more conspicuous ; the upper tail-coverts brown ; the wings are browner, the primary-coverts black ; the head is feathered, not bare on the crown ; the only bare parts are round the eyes, a yellow patch behind the latter, and the sides

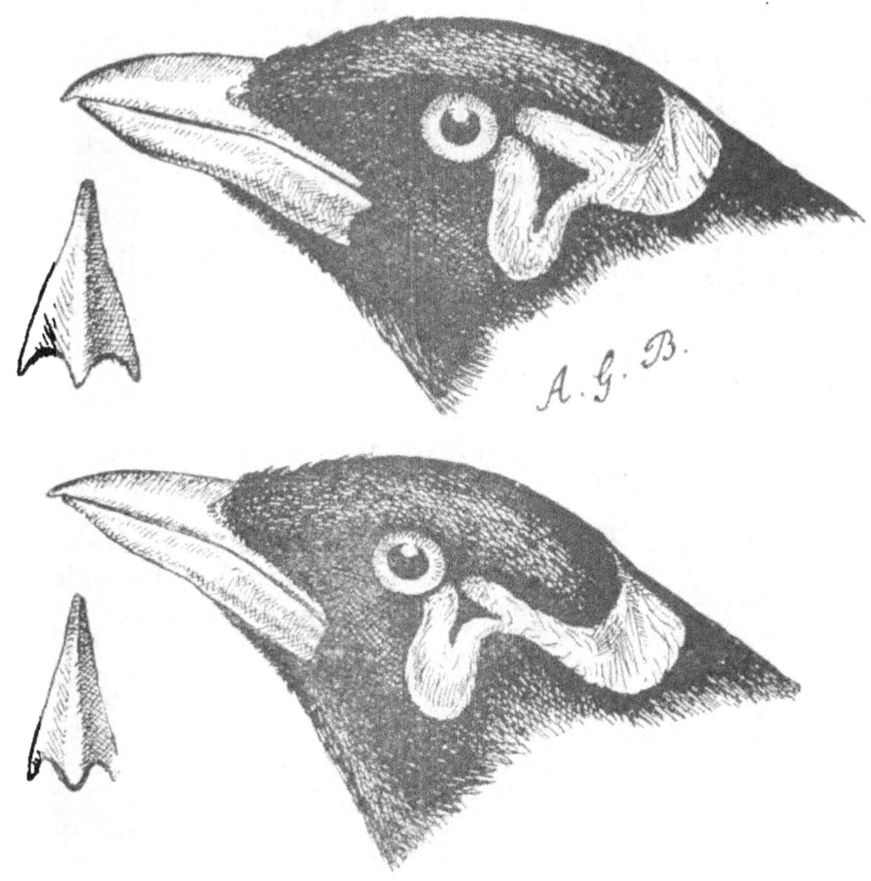

MALE AND FEMALE OF THE GREATER HILL-MYNAH.

of the throat ; the lores are dusky ; sides of face and under parts buffish, whiter on the centre of abdomen. The male has two erect wattles on the centre of the crown and a pendant wattle in the centre of the face. I have never seen the Javan Mynah in the market or at shows, but it has been represented at our Zoological Gardens.

Greater Hill-Mynah (*Mainatus intermedius*).

The female is smaller than the male, but similar in colouring ; her bill is considerably weaker.

LESSER HILL-MYNAH (*Mainatus religiosus*).

As with the preceding, the difference, apart from form of bill, seems to consist chiefly in the inferior size of the female and her shorter wing.

Glossy Starlings (*Lamprocolius, etc.*).

GREEN GLOSSY STARLING (*Lamprocolius chalybeus*).

PURPLE-HEADED GLOSSY STARLING (*Lamprocolius purpureus*).

The only sexual difference indicated for these two species is that the males are generally larger than the females.

LONG-TAILED GLOSSY STARLING.
(*Photograph by Miss Alderson.*)

RUFOUS-VENTED GLOSSY STARLING
(*Spreo pulcher*)

The female is noticeably smaller than the male.

LONG-TAILED GLOSSY STARLING
(*Lamprotornis caudatus*).

Although no sexual difference has been indicated, there can be little doubt that the female is smaller than the male.

In all the true Starlings, in addition to the differences above noted, the bills of the sexes should be compared; for, although the sexual characters are not so well defined in the bills of *Sturnidæ* (*Mainatus* excepted) as in many other families, the longer and somewhat more slender type of bill would always be likely to indicate a cock bird.

Bower-Birds (*Ptilonorhynchidæ*).

SATIN BOWER-BIRD (*Ptilonorhynchus violaceus*).

The female is smaller than the male, has a shorter wing; her prevalent colour is greyish-green, instead of black shot with Prussian-blue, with cinnamon on the outer part of the wing, golden brownish tail-feathers, somewhat ashy ear-coverts, slightly brownish throat, and the rest of the under parts somewhat yellowish, all the feathers being crossed by blackish bars, some of them with a looped inner

THE BOWER-BIRD.

F

stripe bounding the shaft for some distance and then uniting across it. I have not noticed this chararter in young birds, which also are less sharply barred, and show indications of pale spots inside the outer bar of the feathers; they are not blotched with black, even in male birds, until the change to adult plumage has commenced.

Australian Cat-Bird (*Æluroedus viridis*).

The sexes of what the Zoological Society calls the "Green Bower-Birds" have not been differentiated in the Museum Catalogue, but I should expect to find a shorter wing in the female than in the male.

Spotted Bower-Bird (*Chlamydodera maculata*).

The female is smaller than the male, has no lilac band on the nape, and has faint dusky bars on the under parts.

Regent-Bird (*Sericulus melinus*).

Dr Sharpe thus describes the female: "Different from the male. General colour above brown, mottled with white centres to the feathers, edged with black; scapulars like the back; wing-coverts and quills plain brown, the latter dusky brown on the inner webs; the innermost secondaries with an irregular white spot at the tip; upper tail-coverts brown, more dusky on the inner web; forehead light brown, mottled with minute dusky tips to the feathers; hinder crown and occiput black; sides of head, eyebrow, and nape reddish-brown, mottled with dusky edges to the feathers; hind neck whitish, with dusky margins, followed by a patch of black across the lower hind neck; lores and base of forehead buffy-whitish; cheeks reddish-brown, like the sides of the face; chin and sides of throat light reddish, with the centre and lower part of throat black; remainder of under surface of body whity-brown, uniform on the abdomen, the breast and sides of the body spotted with blackish-brown margins to the feathers; the thighs and under tail-coverts reddish-brown; under wing-coverts and axillaries like the breast, and barred across with dusky brown; quills brown below, light reddish along the inner web" (*Catalogue of Birds*, vol. vi. p. 396).

Dr Sharpe makes the female an inch longer than the male, and its wing a quarter of an inch longer; this difference in length of wing would probably not compensate for the extra weight which it would have to support, and thus the male would still have the advantage when flying.

The Paradise Birds (*Paradiseidæ*), when imported, are so expensive that I hardly think it advisable to consider them in the present treatise. I shall therefore proceed direct to the *Corvidæ*.

Chapter XVI.

CROW-LIKE BIRDS (*Corvidæ*).

A PERSONAL examination of various genera and species of this family has convinced me that I have been quite wrong in accepting as correct the statements of even scientific ornithologists respecting the form of the bill in the Crows; it only proves once more that if you wish to arrive at the exact truth you must not accept even the *dicta* of the most reliable without the convincing evidence of your own eyesight.

The sexual differences in the bills of the *Corvidæ* are almost invariably of the same nature as in the Thrushes, and not the reverse, as I had been led to believe by the positive assertions of Stevenson and others, the males (not the females) being generally characterised by a longer and more slender form of bill. In most species this is a well-marked character, though in typical *Corvus*, or *Corone* (as the genus is sometimes called), the difference between the sexes is less strongly defined than in most of the other genera.

It will, I think, be more convenient to note the English and foreign species under each genus :—

The Choughs (*Pyrrhocorax*).

COMMON CHOUGH (*Pyrrhocorax graculus*).

The female has a shorter and slightly thicker bill than the male; she is also a trifle smaller.

ALPINE CHOUGH (*Pyrrhocorax alpinus*).

In this short-billed species the sexual differences are similar in character to those of the preceding.

NUTCRACKER (*Nucifraga caryocatactes*).

Contrary to Stevenson's statement, the bill of the male is longer and rather more slender than that of the female; she is also a rather smaller bird, and her wings are a little browner. Some males have a tawny suffusion on the spots on the breast, but this may be an inconstant character.

THE COMMON JAY.

The Jays.

COMMON JAY (*Garrulus glandarius*).

The female chiefly differs from the male in its distinctly broader and shorter bill. This character also serves to distinguish the other species of the genus.

BLUE JAY (*Cyanocitta cristata*).

The bill of the female is distinctly shorter than that of the male, and, when viewed in profile, is seen to be noticeably deeper. This difference will also serve to separate the sexes of other species in this genus.

BLUE-BEARDED JAY (*Cyanocorax cyanopogon*).

I could discover no sexed specimens in the British Museum series, but the sexes doubtless differ, as in the following :—

PILEATED JAY (*Cyanocorax chrysops*).*

When viewed from above, the bill of the female is distinctly broader than that of the male, but there seems little, if any, difference in its length.

* This is the scientific name given to the species in the Museum Catalogue.

CANADA JAY (*Perisoreus infaustus*).

The bill of the female is heavier and shorter than that of the male. As with the preceding Jays, there is little, if any, difference of plumage between the sexes.

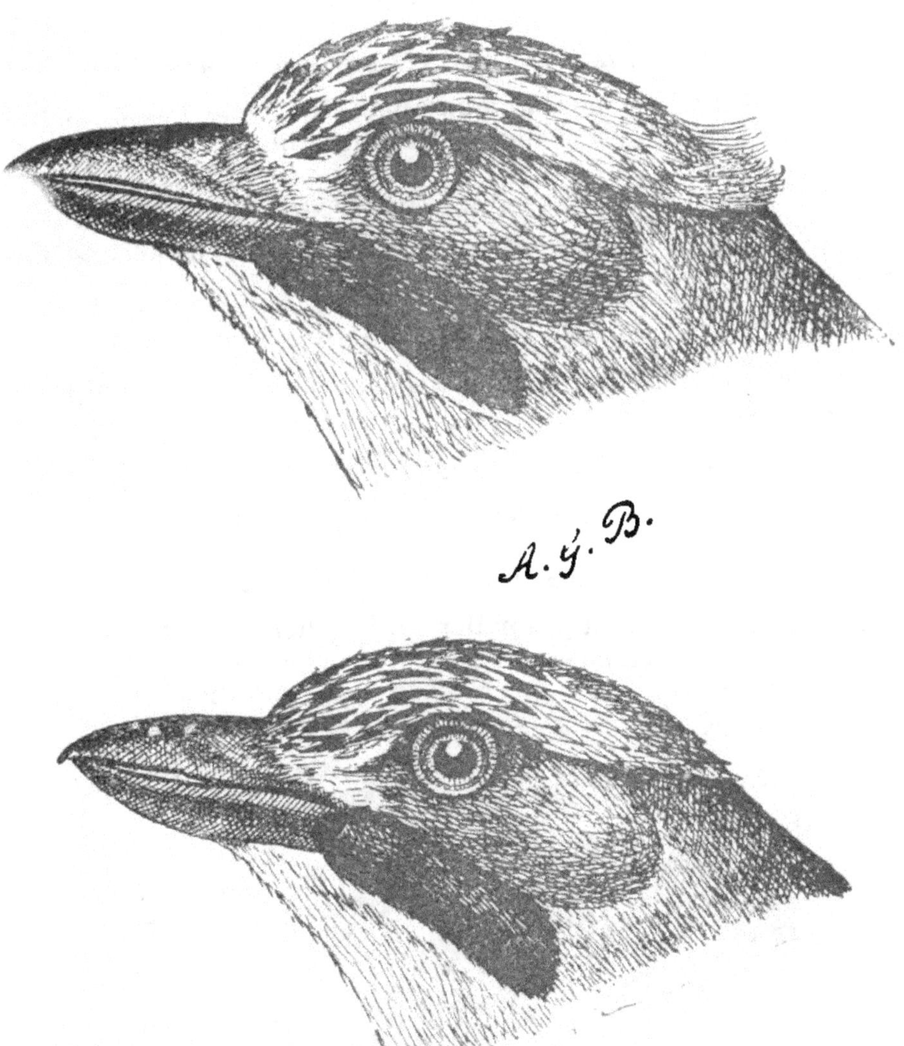

HEAD OF MALE AND FEMALE ENGLISH JAY.

The Pies.

CHINESE BLUE PIE (*Urocissa sinensis*).

The female is smaller than the male, and her bill is shorter and heavier in character.

OCCIPITAL BLUE PIE (*Urocissa occipitalis*).

In this species the bill of the female is far stronger than that of the male.

How to Sex Cage Birds.

Hunting Cissa (*Cissa venatoria*).

Here, again, the female has the stronger bill.

Wandering Tree-Pie (*Dendrocitta rufa*).

The female is browner than the male, and has a much stronger bill.

Chinese Tree-Pie (*Dendrocitta sinensis*).

This species is somewhat abnormal, the male having a slightly heavier bill than the female; he has more blue in his plumage.

Himalayan Tree-Pie (*Dendrocitta himalayensis*).

The female is generally less grey than the male, and has the heavier bill.

Chinese Blue Magpie (*Cyanopolius cyanus*).

In the female the bill is much shorter and less pointed than that of the male.

Spanish Blue Magpie (*Cyanopolius cooki*).

The bills of the sexes differ as in the preceding species.

Common Magpie (*Pica rustica*).

The female is slightly smaller and duller than the male, has a shorter and distinctly heavier bill.

Magpie

Himalayan Magpie (*Pica bottanensis*).

The bills of the sexes differ as in the preceding species.

Chinese Magpie (*Pica sericea*).

The same note applies to this as to the preceding.

Typical Crows (*Corvus*).

Jackdaw (*Corvus monedula*).

The female is slightly smaller than the male, the bill is a trifle shorter, the grey patch on the nape smaller and duller.

Raven (*Corvus corax*).

The female is smaller than the male, with slightly shorter bill, and the plumage less distinctly shot with purple and blue.

Indian Crow (*Corvus splendens*).

The sexes differ much as in the Raven.

Australian Crow (*Corvus australis*).

The same remark applies to this as to the preceding. Gould tells us that some specimens have white and others brown irides, but whether this is a sexual distinction or due to age does not appear. As we know that the English Jay when young has blue irides but afterwards they become vinous-brownish, it seems probable that the birds with white irides may be immature.

Carrion Crow (*Corvus corone*).

Judging from an examination of the Museum skins, the bill of the male in this species is remarkable for being slightly heavier and shorter than that of the female. The plumage is a trifle more glossy, but does not seem to differ in other respects.

Hooded Crow (*Corvus cornix*).

The female is slightly smaller than the male; the bill a trifle longer, as in *C. corone*, but with heavier lower mandible, and broader throughout when viewed from above; the mantle and back are rather browner (less ashy) than in the male.

White-necked Crow (*Corvus scapulatus*).

The sexes are much alike, but the female is perhaps a trifle smaller and duller in colouring, with shorter but heavier bill.

Rook (*Corvus frugilegus*).

The female is slightly smaller and less glossy than the male.

We now come to the Crow-Shrikes, Piping-Crows, and Butcher-Crows, which have been placed near the Shrikes, but which the Zoological Society of London still regards as aberrant *Corvidæ*. As with the latter birds, the female usually has the shorter and stouter bill.

Crow-Shrikes (*Strepera*).

Pied Crow-Shrike (*Strepera graculina*).

Sexes remarkably similar in plumage, but the female is always a trifle smaller than the male. The same remark applies to the Sooty Crow-Shrike (*S. fuliginosa*); but, according to Gould, no such difference exists between the sexes of the Hill Crow-Shrike (*S. arguta*) and the Grey Crow-Shrike (*S. anaphonensis*), which he says can only be sexed by dissection. He probably never compared the outline of the bills of male and female, or failed to recognise its importance.

Piping Crows (*Gymnorhina*).

White-backed Piping-Crow (*Gymnorhina leuconota*).

The female of this species has a shorter and stouter bill than the male; the nape, back, and rump ash-grey; the back and rump with blackish shaft-streaks and mottled white tips to the feathers. I take this description from an old female sent to me in the flesh, and it nearly approaches other examples in the Museum collection which

THE RAVEN.

(probably in consequence of Gould's note on the immature bird) are regarded as young examples.

Tasmanian Piping-Crow (*Gymnorhina organica*).

"The female differs in having the nape of the neck and back grey, and the primaries and tips of the tail-feathers brownish-black" (Gould, *Handbook of Birds of Australia*, vol. i. p. 179). Gadow, who asserts that the sexes of *G. leuconota* are "exactly alike in plumage," regards the Tasmanian bird as a mere smaller form, in which case Gould's distinction confirms mine.

Black-backed Piping-Crow (*Gymnorhina tibicen*).

No sexual difference has been noted, but I should expect an authenticated female to be browner than the male and the back grey mottled, as recorded for the young bird. Undoubtedly the bills of the sexes differ in length and depth.

Butcher-Crows (*Cracticus*).

Long-billed Butcher-Crow (*Cracticus destructor*).

"*Female.*—Rather browner than the male, and generally of a more dingy appearance; body below more uniformly tinged with pale brownish-grey on the sides of breast; flanks pale brownish-grey" (Gadow, *Catalogue of Birds*, vol. viii. p. 100).

Pied Butcher-Crow (*Cracticus picatus*).

No distinction has been indicated between the sexes; it will therefore be necessary to compare the outline of the bill in order to pick out a pair.

Chapter XVII.

LARKS (*Alaudidæ*).

In the soaring birds of this family one expects to find the wings of the males disproportionately long and powerful, and the chest consequently broader than in the females. This is undoubtedly the case in *Alauda, Galerita, Calendula, Mirafra, Melanocorypha*, and *Otocorys;* but probably not in *Rhamphocorys* and *Pyrrhulauda;* while in *Calandrella* the wing and tail are longer in the female, and in *Alaudula* the wing of the female appears to be proportionately shorter than that of the male, and the tail much shorter.

As a general rule, therefore, it will be seen that the male bird is undoubtedly more powerful on the wing, so that the proportions of wing and chest measurement offer good characters for distinguishing

THE COMMON SKYLARK.

the sexes of the Larks, apart from any other characters which may exist.   The length of the hind claw is said to differ sexually.

As in the Zoological Society's List and Howard Saunder's Manual, as also in *British Birds, with their Nests and Eggs*, I have left this family next to the Crows, although its relationships are rather with the Pipits and Finches.

COMMON SKYLARK (*Alauda arvensis*).

The sexes do not differ in plumage, but the female is smaller, and has proportionately shorter wings, the average length of the male being 7 inches, and its wing $4\frac{1}{2}$ inches; that of the female $6\frac{1}{2}$ inches, and its wing $4\frac{1}{10}$ inches.

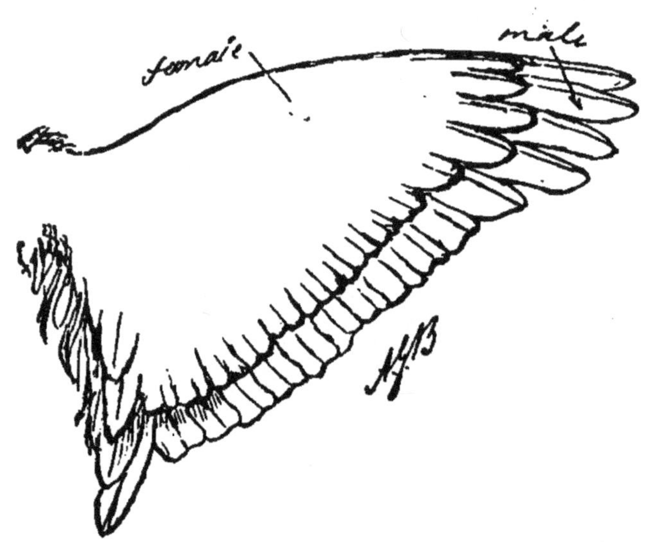

SHOWING RELATIVE SIZES IN MALE AND FEMALE OF THE SKYLARK.

INDIAN SKYLARK (*Alauda gulgula*).

In addition to its slightly inferior size, much shorter wing, and slightly shorter tail, the female differs from the male in its dusky claws and darker eyes.

Dr Sharpe considers the Sweet-voiced Lark (*Alauda cœlivox*) to be simply a pale Chinese race of the Indian Skylark; he has removed the Woodlark and Crested Lark from the genus *Alauda* to *Lullula* and *Galerita*, but has not been generally followed in the case of the Woodlark.

WOODLARK (*Alauda arborea*).

The sexes differ very slightly in size, but the average length of the wing in the female is decidedly shorter.

CRESTED LARK (*Galerita cristata*).

The female resembles the male in plumage, but is smaller, and has a much shorter wing.

Thick-billed Lark (*Calendula crassirostris*).

"The sexes are alike in colour, but the female has rather a smaller bill. The wing appears to be from 3·95 to 4·1 in the males, and from 3·75 to 3·9 in the females" (Sharpe, *Catalogue of Birds*, vol. xiii p. 640).

Madras Bush-Lark (*Mirafra affinis*).

The sexes are alike in plumage, but the female is smaller, and has a shorter wing; as the tail also is a good bit shorter, the body of the female would be almost as long as that of the male, and therefore would be heavier in proportion to the size of the wings.

Tientsin or Mongolian Lark (*Melanocorypha mongolica*).

Dr Sharpe states that, unfortunately, none of the Museum specimens are sexed as females, but the larger birds are sexed as males; he gives the wing measurements as from 4·9 to 5·0 inches, and from 5·25 to 5·4 inches, and thinks that the former are probably female birds; there cannot be much doubt of this.

Calandra Lark (*Melanocorypha calandra*).

In addition to its smaller size and considerably shorter wing, "the female is generally more rufous than the male, and has the throat more plentifully spotted with black, and the black patch on the sides of the neck is smaller" (Sharpe, *Catalogue of Birds*, vol. xiii. p. 553).

Black Lark (*Melanocorypha yeltoniensis*).

In addition to its much smaller size and shorter wing, the female differs from the male in being more like the preceding species. Dr Sharpe describes it as follows:—"Ochreous-brown, with dark centres to the feathers, the crown mottled with black; quills blackish, with whity-brown edges, whiter on the primaries, under-surface of body white, with a sandy-buff tinge on the throat; the fore-neck, breast, and sides of body spotted with black, some of the markings longitudinal and even spear-shaped, the flanks especially streaked" (*Catalogue of Birds*, vol. xiii. p. 560).

Shore-Lark (*Otocoris alpestris*).

In addition to its smaller size and shorter wing, the female in summer plumage is browner than the male, and less tinted with vinous; the black band on the crown less prominent; the back of the crown and the nape brown, the latter and the back more distinctly marked with dark brown than in the male; the black on the sides of the face and throat less pronounced, and the fore-head and throat, which are white in the male. are yellowish in the female.

The White-bellied Shore-Lark (*O. chrysolæma*), being a native of Cuba, is not frequently imported as a cage-bird.

Algerian Shore-Lark (*Otocorys bilopha*).

The Museum appears not to possess sexed examples, but there is no doubt that the structural differences are similar to those in the European species.

Clot-bey Lark (*Rhamphocorys clot-bey*).

As the Museum Catalogue does not distinguish the sexes of this bird, and it does not come into Shelley's *Birds of Africa*, I asked Mr Seth-Smith to look it up in his copy of Whitaker's *Birds of Tunisia*, and he courteously forwarded the following extract:— "Adult female paler than the male and more uniformly isabelline in its coloration, with less black on the under parts, and slightly smaller in size" (vol. i. p. 288).

I don't suppose either of the preceding birds is very frequently imported.

White-headed Bullfinch Lark (*Pyrrhulauda verticalis*).

Captain Shelley describes no differences of measurement in the sexes. Being essentially a ground-bird, chiefly taking to flight when alarmed, one would hardly expect it to develop its wings and chest-muscles like the soaring Larks. Unlike the cock, which has a black head, Captain Shelley thus describes the hen: "Above pale sandy brown, with a few dark shaft-stripes on the crown; back, wings, and tail as in the males: only the axillaries and under wing-coverts are more dusky, and the latter have a broad outer band of buff, sides of head buff, with broad pale brown shaft-stripes to the ear-coverts; throat white; under surface of body buff, with a few brown shaft-stripes" (*Birds of Africa*, vol. iii. p. 84).

Short-toed Lark (*Calandrella brachydactyla*).

The sexes are of the same length, but both wing and tail in the hen are longer than in the cock. This would certainly give her the advantage in flight, so that one would expect migrating flocks of hens to arrive at their breeding-grounds earlier than the cocks, and that they selected their husbands rather than the reverse. In addition to these structural differences, Dr Sharpe says that *C. brachydactyla* female differs from the male in having "hardly any streaks on the fore-neck, the lateral patch on which is also smaller" (*Catalogue of Birds*, vol. xiii. p. 582).

Andalusian Short-toed Lark (*Alaudula bœtica*).

Seebohm and Sharpe both regard this as a race of *A. pispoletta*, the Short-toed Lark of Asia Minor, Southern Russia, and Central Asia. The female differs from the male in being slightly smaller, but with the same length of wing and a much shorter tail; in plumage she appears not to differ.

To render this series of articles fairly complete, it will be necessary just to glance at the Pittas, Tyrants, and one or two other groups, members of which are not infrequently imported, before proceeding to the Picarian groups.

Pittas (*Pittidæ*).

Jerdon regarded these birds as Ground-Thrushes.

BENGAL PITTA (*Pitta brachyura*).

Unlike the Thrushes, the bill of the male is very slightly shorter and stouter than that of the female. In the latter sex the lower mandible is much paler than in the male, and the rami, viewed from below, are seen to be much more divergent.

NOISY PITTA (*Pitta strepitans*).

The Museum specimens are not sexed, but what I take to be males have a rather heavier and longer bill than the supposed females; and the scarlet on the lower abdomen and under tail-coverts is much brighter and less diffused.

The Tyrants (*Tyrannidæ*).

The two species most frequently imported are much alike in colouring, but differ greatly in form of bill. Their general aspect and their habits are similar to those of Kingfishers.

PITANGUA OR BROAD-BILLED TYRANT (*Megarhynchus pitangus*).

When viewed from above, the bill of the female is slightly shorter than that of the male, and distinctly broader at base; the sides therefore are far more oblique; the throat is of a less pure white colour, and the tail longer.

SULPHURY TYRANT (*Pitangus sulphuratus*).

The bill of the male is considerably longer than in the female, is narrower at base, and less acute at tip; the borders to the flight-feathers are also of a distinctly deeper cinnamon-reddish in the male than in the female.

Oven-Birds (*Dendrocolaptidæ*).

RED OVEN-BIRD (*Furnarius rufus*).

Comparing fully adult birds, the female is a trifle smaller than the male; she has a very slightly shorter and more slender bill; her throat is not quite of so pure a white, and the centre of her abdomen is more stained with brownish.

HEAD OF MALE AND FEMALE OF THE GREEN WOODPECKER.

CHAPTER XVIII.

WE now come to the order *Picariæ*, which includes the Swifts, Goat-suckers, Woodpecker-like birds, Kingfishers, Rollers, Bee-Eaters, Hoopoes, Cuckoos, etc. Of the first two, I think one need take no notice; for although I once succeeded in keeping a Swift alive for a month, and the European Goatsucker has once been kept and exhibited in Germany, neither of these birds can fairly be regarded as cage-birds. I shall therefore proceed at once to the,—

WOODPECKER-LIKE BIRDS (*Picidæ*).

Wrynecks (*Iynginæ*).

COMMON WRYNECK (*Iynx torquilla*).

The female is distinctly smaller than the male, has a shorter and weaker bill; the feathers of the upper parts tipped with pale sandy brown, and narrowly barred with black; nape and scapulars without black streaks; ground colour of the wings sandy brown, instead of dull tawny; the throat and breast without tawny suffusion.

Woodpeckers (*Picinæ*).

GREEN WOODPECKER (*Gecinus viridis*).

In birds of this type, which are always using their bills for hacking holes in trees, one would hardly expect to find much sexual difference in this part of their structure. In the Green Woodpecker the bill of the male is a trifle shorter than that of the female, but the difference of plumage in these birds is the easiest guide to follow. The female of *G. viridis* has less carmine on the crown than the cock, and none on the cheeks.

GREAT SPOTTED WOODPECKER (*Dendrocopus major*).

The female is rather smaller than the male, and has no crimson on the nape.

LESSER SPOTTED WOODPECKER (*Dendrocopus minor*).

The female has the crown white, and the under parts are more streaked than in the male. When quite young the female has the front of the crown crimson.

BANDED WOODPECKER (*Centurus tricolor*).

The female is smaller than the male; her bill is shorter, and broader at the base. Instead of the crimson on the crown, this part of the head in the female is buffish-brown in front shading into ashy-brown tinged with yellowish at the back, and is bounded behind by a red diffused border on the nape.

RED-HEADED WOODPECKER (*Melanerpes erythrocephalus*).

The female is slightly smaller than the male, and her bill appears to be rather longer, and is distinctly more slender.

WHITE-HEADED WOODPECKER (*Melanerpes candidus*).

The bill of the female is shorter, and less slender towards the tip than that of the male. She also differs from the latter sex in wanting the yellow band on the nape, which is white like the head.

GOLDEN-WINGED WOODPECKER (*Colaptes auratus*).

The female is smaller than the male; her bill is shorter and more slender, and she has no black moustachial streak from the bill across the cheek.

Colies (*Coliidæ*).

These interesting long-tailed birds are not very freely imported; but as it is to be hoped that the rapid increase in the numbers of aviculturists in this country will induce dealers to import these and many others of the smaller aviary birds more freely, I think it will be useful to point out the differences by which the sexes may be distinguished.

CHESTNUT-BACKED COLY (*Colius castanonotus*).

In the Museum series I could find no male sex-marks on any of the specimens, but one example sexed as a female was conspicuously larger than all the others, had a much longer tail, and a more curved upper mandible.

RED-CHEEKED COLY (*Colius erythromelon*).

The female is smaller than the male, and has a smaller beak. In colouring it only differs in being slightly paler.

BLACK-NECKED COLY (*Colius nigricollis*).

I found only one female bearing the sex-mark, but the differences are probably similar to those in the following species.

STRIATED COLY (*Colius striatus*).

The female has a longer and broader beak than the male. The upper mandible is also more curved, as in *C. castanonotus.* The crown of the head is paler, rather more ashy.

CAPE COLY (*Colius capensis*).

The female is larger than the male; her beak is longer and more tapering. It will be seen from the foregoing that the sexes of the Colies differ very little in plumage, so that the size and the form of the beak are of considerable importance.

Kingfishers (*Alcedinidæ*).

Although the European Kingfisher is not the most satisfactory bird to keep in a cage or small aviary, it has been successfully kept by various aviculturists. In an extensive aviary enclosing water well stocked with small fish it should be possible to breed it. The foreign Kingfishers, however, are more easily kept in captivity.

EUROPEAN KINGFISHER (*Alcedo ispida*).

The female is slightly smaller than the male, and has a more slender bill, the under surface of which is largely coloured red instead of black.

LAUGHING KINGFISHERS.
(From a Photograph by Messrs Kerry, of Sydney.)

WHITE-BREASTED KINGFISHER (*Halcyon smyrnensis*).

The bill of the female is considerably broader from the base to the third fourth than in the male, and is noticeably shorter. I can discover no constant difference in plumage.

SACRED KINGFISHER (*Halcyon sancta*).

The bill of the female is slightly longer than that of the male, and tapers more gradually. When viewed from above it is seen to be not so full in the middle. This sex is altogether duller than the male, more olive above and on the breast, which is of a pale brownish rather than buffish tint; the feathers retain the dusky fringes characteristic of the young plumage.

NEW ZEALAND KINGFISHER (*Halcyon vagans*).

A larger and duller representative of *H. sancta*. The female has a much longer and more regularly tapering bill than the male, and a much less vivid blue-green eyebrow streak. The breast feathers, especially at the sides, are partly fringed with dark brown, but less strongly than in young birds.

LAUGHING KINGFISHER (*Dacelo gigas*).

The bill of the female is remarkably shorter than that of the male, and is much broader at two-thirds from its base. I can discover no constant difference of plumage.

The allied *Dacelo cervina* and *D. leachii*, though both more beautiful in colouring than the common Laughing Kingfisher (or "Jackass," as it is frequently called), are rarely imported, so that it is not necessary to do more than suggest that anybody who wishes to sex them should compare the length and outline of the bills.

I do not propose to regard the Hornbills as cage-birds. They are only suitable for large aviaries.

EUROPEAN KINGFISHER.

Chapter XIX.

TOUCANS AND OTHER PICARIANS.

Of the remaining *Picariæ* which it will be necessary to deal with are the Hoopoes, Bee-Eaters, Rollers, Toucans and allies, Barbets, and Touracous. The Motmots are beautiful birds, but very rarely imported; Cuvier's Podargus and the Oil-Bird need not be considered. The Cuckoos generally are most unsatisfactory as cage-birds, the European and Guira Cuckoos being more frequently met with than others, but neither of them is likely to become very popular.

THE COMMON HOOPOE.

Hoopoes (*Upupidæ*).

COMMON HOOPOE (*Upupa epops*).

The female is rather smaller than the male, has a much shorter wing, bill, and crest, so that there need never be the least difficulty in distinguishing her.

Bee-Eaters (*Meropidæ*).

COMMON BEE-EATER (*Merops apiaster*).

The female is rather duller in colouring than the male, and has the two central tail-feathers shorter. Mr R. Phillipps notes the absence of yellow from the forehead in this sex.

Rollers (*Coraciidæ*).

COMMON ROLLER (*Coracias garrulus*).

The female is smaller than the male, and has a smaller and shorter bill; her colouring is slightly duller. In a female in the Museum, which may possibly be in immature plumage, the rump is of a greenish-turquoise colour instead of the usual dull violet, the upper tail-coverts silvery bluish-green instead of the usual dull dark green with pale borders.

We now come to the Toucans, a group of gaudily-coloured birds with very ungainly bills. Many of them are very large, and consequently require spacious cages. They fetch high prices, and yet, I believe, do not remain long on the hands of the dealers.

In order to illustrate to some extent the different character of the bill in the sexes, I have sketched the sexes of one of the smaller species (*Selenidera maculirostris*) in outline, but in some of the largest imported species of *Rhamphastos* the differences are considerably more marked.

OUTLINES OF HEADS OF MALE AND FEMALE OF *Selenidera maculirostris* TO ILLUSTRATE THE SEXUAL DIFFERENCES IN THE BEAKS OF TOUCANS.

Toucans (*Rhamphastidæ*).

Toco Toucan (*Rhamphastos toco*).

In fully adult specimens the bill of the male is at least one inch longer than that of the female and a trifle broader at base. As with most of the Toucans, the sexes do not differ appreciably in plumage.

Sulphur-breasted Toucan (*Rhamphastos carinatus*).

The female is much smaller than the male, and has an altogether shorter and more abruptly terminated bill.

SHORT-BILLED TOUCAN (*Rhamphastos brevicarinatus*).

The female is smaller than the male; her bill is considerably shorter, with the culmen (ridge) more arched, but the terminal hook shorter and more abruptly formed.

DOUBTFUL TOUCAN (*Rhamphastos tocard*).

I could not discover any examples with the female sex-mark in the series at the Natural History Museum; but I have little doubt that the smaller birds, with much shorter and less tapering bills, represent that sex.

RED-BILLED TOUCAN (*Rhamphastos erythrorhynchus*).

The female is smaller than the male, and her bill is distinctly shorter and less curved at the tip.

CUVIER'S TOUCAN (*Rhamphastos cuvieri*).

In the Museum series of skins I could discover no example with the female sex-mark; but this species is certain to differ sexually in the same manner as its allies.

ARIEL TOUCAN (*Rhamphastos ariel*).

In the female the bill is slightly shorter than in the male, with shorter terminal curvature. In the specimens which I compared, the flattened basal portion of the culmen was twice as wide in the female as in the male. I am, however, doubtful as to the value of this as a distinctive character; it seems possible that it may be merely an indication of age. With a large series of sexed specimens alone could one definitely decide upon the constancy of a character of this nature.

SULPHUR-AND-WHITE-BREASTED TOUCAN (*Rhamphastos vitellinus*).

The female is smaller than the male, and has a considerably shorter bill.

GREEN-BILLED TOUCAN (*Rhamphastos dicolorus*).

By a comparison of specimens labelled as male and female in the Museum series, one is forced to the conclusion that the usual sexual differences in the structure of the bill are reversed in this species.

MAXIMILIAN'S ARACARI (*Pteroglossus wiedi*).

The female is a little smaller than the male, and has a rather smaller bill. I noted also that the blackish dorsal stripe on the culmen of the bill was wider, especially towards the base, in the female; but whether this is a fairly constant character or not can only be satisfactorily settled by a comparison of many sexed examples.

Banded Aracari (*Pteroglossus torquatus*).

The female is very slightly smaller than the male, and has a considerably shorter bill, with less curved tip.　In the sexed specimens, I found the black dorsal stripe narrower in the female, but much more elongated.　This curious departure from the type of marking found in the preceding species seems to me to indicate that the character of the dorsal stripe must be variable, and therefore unreliable.

Spot-billed Toucanet (*Selenidera maculirostris*).

The female is smaller than the male; her bill is shorter, less tapering, but with more pronounced terminal hook.　The banding of the bill is very variable, but the plumage of the sexes in this species differs considerably.　All the steel-black areas in the male plumage are replaced by vinous-chestnut in the female, this colouring being paler and clearer on the throat and breast than on the upper surface.　The broad streak across the lower portion of the ear-coverts, which is orange and yellow in the male, is replaced by a narrower green streak in the female.

A comparison of the characters indicated above will tend to show that, as a general rule, male Toucans (including Aracaris and Toucanets) are larger than their mates, and have longer and more tapering bills.　Whether there is any difference in the colouring of the iris in the sexes has not been stated, therefore there probably is none; but the soft parts in birds have received so much less attention than ought to be paid to them by collectors, that the colouring of the eyes and other soft parts in living specimens is always worth noting and recording.　In the case of some of the nearly related Doves (the local races of the Passerine Dove, for instance), the differences in the colouring of the soft parts are very remarkable, and are, to my mind, quite as worthy to be regarded as having a specific signification as modifications in plumage.

Barbets (*Capitonidæ*).

In these gaudy birds the plumage of the sexes is much alike, but the form of the bill differs.

Blue-cheeked Barbet (*Cyanops asiatica*).

In the female the bill is a trifle shorter and broader, and its culmen, viewed in profile, is seen to be slightly more arched than in the male.　She appears to be rather larger than her mate, but with shorter wing and tail.

Hodgson's Barbet (*Cyanops lineata*).

The size of both sexes in this bird appears to vary greatly, but the female has decidedly the broader bill.

GREAT BARBET (*Megalæma virens*).

Unlike the preceding species, the female of *M. virens* is smaller than the male, with slightly longer wing but shorter tail.

PURPLE BARBET (*Trachyphonus purpuratus*).

The bill of the female is much shorter and broader than that of the male.

I do not propose to consider the Cuckoos as cage-birds, as already stated.

The Touracous are large, showy birds, often kept in cage and aviary, but more particularly in public gardens. They differ very little sexually as regards plumage. In the Museum series I found comparatively few examples bearing sex-marks, but in each case I noted that the beak of the female was quite conspicuously shorter than that of the male.

SENEGAL TOURACOU (*Turacus persa*).

The female appears to be larger than the male.

BUFFON'S TOURACOU (*Turacus buffoni*).

I noted nothing beyond the much shorter beak of the female.

LIVINGSTONE'S TOURACOU (*Turacus livingstonii*).

In sexed examples from Nyassaland, the male was more golden green on mantle and wings than the female; the feathers of the mantle fringed with gold instead of blue.

I think it would be waste of space to mention more of these birds in detail, as there will be no difficulty in sexing any of them by a comparison of the beaks.

CHAPTER XX.

KA-KAS AND LORIES.

WE now come to the *Psittaci*, or Parrots, the sexes of which are not always easy to recognise, though if the late Mr Abraham's distinction is constant, and he showed it to me in the sexed skulls of at least half a dozen widely different groups of Parrots, one ought always to be able to tell the sex by feeling the hinder angle of the lower jaw, which is more pointed, and developed farther backward in the female than the male, thus giving space for the attachment of a more powerful muscle, which will account for the fact that the bite even of a female Budgerigar will draw blood, whereas that of a male of the same species will not.

In addition to this character, the females of many of the Parrots are smaller than the males, and have rounder heads; in some, the iris is paler in the females, and it is probable, if careful measurements were taken, that most of them have shorter wings than their mates; in some the bare patches on the face differ sexually, and, as a matter of course, the form of the beak is always worth comparing, and the colour of the cere at the base of the upper mandible.

The Ka-Kas (*Nestoridæ*).

According to Gould, these strange birds do not move about the earth with the awkward, shambling gait of the more typical Parrots, but by a series of leaps, exactly after the manner of the Crows.

Kea Parrot or Mountain Ka-Ka (*Nestor notabilis*).

I could find no sexed skins of this bird. I probably overlooked them, as a pair is noted in the Catalogue. Count Salvadori says that the female has the tints of the plumage duller than the male, and the dusky marking of the feathers broader. Doubtless it differs also in form of beak, as in the succeeding species.

Common Ka-Ka (*Nestor meridionalis*).

The beak of the male is much larger, and with more curved terminal hook than that of the female.

The Lories (*Loriidæ*).

The sexes of these birds differ very little in plumage, but there is always a more or less well-defined difference in the outline of the beak when viewed from above; as this difference is similar to that which occurs in many of the Finches, I have not thought it worth while to illustrate it.

Red-fronted Lory (*Chalcopsittacus scintillatus*).

The beak of the male is considerably broader than that of the female, and has a longer terminal hook; the colouring of the top of the head is perceptibly brighter in the male, and this appears to be a constant character so far as I could judge by a comparison of the sexed skins in the Museum.

Blue-streaked Lory (*Eos reticulata*).

The beak of the male is distinctly shorter than that of the female, fuller towards the tip, and with a broader terminal hook; the colouring of its head is also unquestionably brighter.

Blue-tailed Lory (*Eos histrio*).

Oddly enough, in this species the male beak is much narrower than that of the female, and has a noticeably shorter terminal hook.

RED LORY (*Eos rubra*).

The beak of the male is distinctly broader at the base than in the female, and the scarlet colouring of the head is brighter.

VIOLET-NECKED LORY (*Eos riciniata*).

In the male the base of the beak is broader than in the female, and the culmen or ridge makes a more perfect arch.

THREE-COLOURED LORY (*Lorius lory*).

The skull of the male appears to be broader than that of the female; the beak is noticeably broader, but appears to vary greatly with age, the largest birds having by far the broadest beaks.

PURPLE-CAPPED LORY (*Lorius domicella*).

I could discover no sexed female; but doubtless the beak of the male is broader at base.

GREEN-TAILED LORY (*Lorius chlorocercus*).

The male beak is broader at the base and rather fuller towards the tip than that of the female.

BLUE-THIGHED LORY (*Lorius tibialis*).

I found only one skin in the Museum, but doubtless the sexes differ as in the allied species.

CHATTERING LORY (*Lorius garrulus*).

I found three sexed males but no sexed females, but it is probable that the beak of the male is broader at base than that of the female.

YELLOW-BACKED LORY (*Lorius flavo-palliatus*).

The base of the beak is broader in the male, and the arch of the culmen greater.

At the commencement of his account of the Lorikeets (*Parrakeets*, p. 3), Mr Seth-Smith observes: "The sexes are, so far as I am aware, alike in plumage in all of the Lories, but, in most cases at least, the females are slightly less in size than the males, and possess a smaller and more effeminate-looking head."

BLUE-FACED LORIKEET (*Trichoglossus hæmatodes*).

I could discover no skins in the Museum series sexed as males; but two sexed as females show remarkable differences in the outline of the beak, and although it is possible that they may be due to age, they are exactly what one would expect in opposite sexes. It is, I think, worthy of note that the brighter-coloured bird, in which, like the other unsexed specimens, the breast is strongly tinged with orange, shows a beak of the male type as they also do, whereas the other, which possesses a beak of the female type, shows hardly a trace of this colouring.

How to Sex Cage Birds.

FORSTEN'S LORIKEET (*Trichoglossus forsteni*).

The beak of the male is broader at the base, and tapers less towards the tip than that of the female.

GREEN-NAPED LORIKEET (*Trichoglossus cyanogrammus*).

I could find no sexed males in the Museum, but what I believe to be birds of that sex differ from the females in having the base of the beak broader.

MITCHELL'S LORIKEET (*Trichoglossus mitchelli*).

The male has a shorter and broader beak than the female, with the culmen more arched.

SWAINSON'S LORIKEET (*Trichoglossus novæ-hollandiæ*).

In the male the beak is broader beyond the middle, and tapers less than that of the female.

ORNAMENTAL LORIKEET (*Trichoglossus ornatus*).

The beak of the male is much longer, and broader towards the tip, than that of the female.

SCALY-BREASTED LORIKEET (*Psitteuteles chlorolepidotus*).

As there was only one sexed female in the collection, I can only recommend lovers of the Parrakeets to sex this species upon the excellent characters indicated by my friend Mr Seth-Smith.

MUSKY LORIKEET (*Glossopsittacus concinnus*).

I went carefully through the long series in the Museum ; but, as with the preceding species, only one female was sexed. I must therefore ask my readers to deal with this species as with *Psitteuteles*. The past generation of collectors of Australian birds seems to have been strangely remiss in labelling specimens with the sex-mark, and yet with birds in which the plumage of the male and female shows very slight shades of difference, it is far more important that the sex should be ascertained by dissection, and carefully noted, than in those where the colouring alone is an ample indication of the sex. Doubtless in the future these drawbacks to study will be abolished ; indeed, when the careful system of measurements of every part now being adopted in the United States becomes general, it will be absolutely necessary that the sex of every specimen shall be recognised. Then, with a large series of males on one side and females on the other, the value of every sexual difference will be appreciated as it has never been up to the present time.

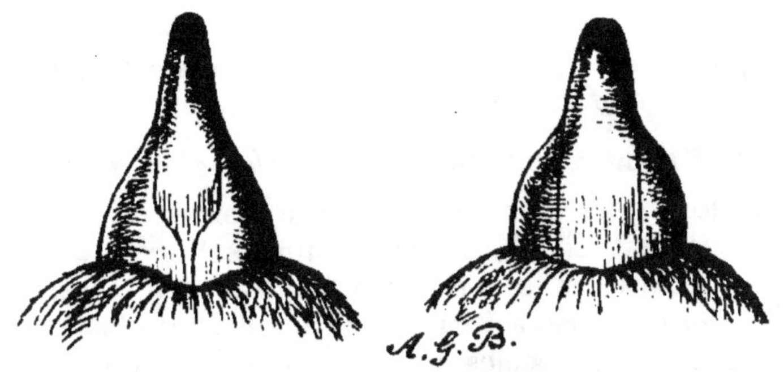

BEAKS OF MALE AND FEMALE OF *Cacatua hæmaturopygia*
WHEN VIEWED FROM ABOVE.

CHAPTER XXI.

THE COCKATOOS (*Cacatuidæ*).

IN these birds the males have the iris of the eye darker than the females.

Subfamily Cacatuinæ (Typical Cockatoos).

The form of the beak, when viewed from above, differs sexually somewhat as in the Lories and Lorikeets.   I give an illustration of *Cacatua hæmaturopygia.*

The Black Cockatoos, though rare in the market and extremely unattractive in appearance, have to be included; indeed, with birds like the Parrots, which are constantly brought home by sailors and many others not specially interested in natural history, it is important not to omit species on account of their present rarity. At any time quite a respectable number may be brought home, and efforts made by lovers of the order to breed them.

GREAT BLACK COCKATOO (*Microglossus aterrimus*).

The beak of the male is much longer and more regularly tapered than that of the female, and the terminal hook is considerably longer.   The female is also a smaller bird.

FUNEREAL COCKATOO (*Calyptorhynchus funereus*).

Specimens not sexed, but probably the structural differences are similar to those of the preceding species.

BANKSIAN COCKATOO (*Calyptorhynchus banksi*).

The female differs from the male as follows :—" Head and upper wing-coverts spotted with yellow ; under surface crossed by narrow irregular bars of pale yellow, which become yellowish-red on the under tail-coverts ; the red part of the tail interrupted by numerous and irregular black bars, and passing into yellowish-red underneath and into sulphur-yellow on the inner margins of the feathers." (Salvadori, *Catalogue of Birds*, vol. xx. p. 110).

WESTERN BLACK COCKATOO (*Calyptorhynchus stellatus*).

Count Salvadori does not describe the sexes of this species; indeed, he tells us that the Museum specimens "are few in number, without having locality or sex marked," but as it appears chiefly to differ from *C. macrorhynchus* in the character of its beak and crest, and the female of that species is said to differ from *C. banksi* in having "the coloured part of the tail mingled yellow and scarlet," we have a guide by which to recognise the sexes.

GANGA COCKATOO (*Callocephalon galeatum*).

The female differs from the male in having "the crest grey; the quills and the tail-feathers with light grey bars; the feathers of the under surface are margined with sulphur-yellow and dull red; the under tail-coverts have dull yellow bars" (Salvadori; *cf.* Gould, *Handbook of Birds of Australia*, ii. p. 30, 1865).

We now come to the White Cockatoos, which are not so easily sexed, but the hens are generally slightly smaller than the cocks, have paler eyes, and a shorter beak, narrower at its base.

GREATER SULPHUR-CRESTED COCKATOO (*Cacatua galerita*).

The female is smaller than the male. Her beak is also shorter, and has a shorter terminal hook.

TRITON COCKATOO (*Cacatua triton*).

The female is smaller than the male. Her beak is smaller, narrower when viewed in profile, with a slightly shorter terminal hook.

LESSER SULPHUR-CRESTED COCKATOO (*Cacatua sulphurea*)

The female is slightly smaller than the male, with a rather shorter and narrower beak (viewed from above), and a shorter terminal hook.

CITRON-CRESTED COCKATOO (*Cacatua citrinocristata*).

Only one female sexed, but the sexual differences would probably be much the same as in the preceding species.

LEADBEATER'S COCKATOO (*Cacatua leadbeateri*).

The male is larger than the female, and has a more finely-formed beak, in which the upper mandible is much narrower, and has a longer terminal hook.

GREATER WHITE-CRESTED COCKATOO (*Cacatua alba*).

In the female the culmen of the beak is much narrower than in the male, and less arched; the terminal hook, viewed in profile, is seen to be narrower towards its base.

BLUE-EYED COCKATOO (*Cacatua ophthalmica*).

There are only sexed females in the Museum series, but the differences will probably be such as in the preceding species.

ROSE-CRESTED COCKATOO (*Cacatua moluccensis*).

Only males are sexed in the Museum, but it is probable that the usual differences exist.

BARE-EYED COCKATOO (*Cacatua gymnopsis*).

Only a female is sexed, but the probable male has a narrower and less arched beak, with a longer and more slender terminal hook.

BLOOD-STAINED COCKATOO (*Cacatua sanguinea*).

The female, as usual, has a shorter and broader beak, with a more heavily-formed terminal hook. It is probable that the cut in the Zoological Society's List is taken from a female.

GOFFIN'S COCKATOO (*Cacatua goffini*).

The female is smaller than the male, and the Museum sexed example has the head, throat, and breast white, the crest slightly yellowish, the beak longer, with more slender terminal hook. Whether the colour differences in the Museum example are constant or not I cannot say, and Count Salvadori does not even mention them. As they are rather striking in a group in which the sexes usually closely resemble one another in plumage, this omission seems somewhat strange.

DUCORPS' COCKATOO (*Cacatua ducorpsi*).

This species seems nearly related to Goffin's Cockatoo. The only sexed male in the Museum has the beak rather badly broken, so that it is difficult to compare it with that of the female. It is, however, evidently broader and altogether larger.

RED-VENTED COCKATOO (*Cacatua hæmaturopygia*).

In the male the beak, viewed from above, is seen to be broader to beyond the middle than that of the female, with a longer and narrower terminal hook.

ROSEATE COCKATOO (*Cacatua roseicapilla*).

The Museum series of this abundant species is unfortunately a very poor one, and only the male is sexed, but the differences are probably similar to those in the preceding species.

SLENDER-BILLED COCKATOO (*Licmetis nasica*).

In the male the beak is noticeably longer, narrower, and generally more slender than that of the female.

WESTERN SLENDER-BILLED COCKATOO (*Licmetis pastinator*).

No examples are recorded in the Museum Catalogue, but the structural differences between the sexes are probably as in the preceding species.

Subfamily Calopsittacinæ (Cockatiels).

THE COCKATIEL (*Calopsittacus novæ-hollandiæ*).

The female is paler and altogether rather browner than the male; the forehead and cheeks only faintly washed with yellow; the lower abdomen and under tail-coverts with dark grey and pale yellow bands, the lower back, upper tail-coverts, and four middle tail-feathers grey with irregular narrow whitish bands; the lateral tail-feathers darker, mottled, and barred with yellow; outer tail-feathers yellow, the inner web irregularly barred with black. Of course there are also differences in the beak, as anyone will discover pretty quickly if he handles both sexes. The bite of the female is distinctly painful.

CHAPTER XXII.

PARROT-LIKE BIRDS (*Psittacidæ*).

Subfamily Conurinæ (Macaws and Conures).

THE Parrotlets and the *Brotogerys* group are also placed in the same subfamily; all the *Conurinæ* are natives of the New World.

HYACINTHINE MACAW (*Anodorhynchus hyacinthinus*).

I found no sexed examples in the Museum, but there is no doubt that the female would be slightly smaller than the male, with a rather smaller and shorter beak, probably rather narrower.

LEAR'S MACAW (*Anodorhynchus leari*).

I only found a sexed male of this species. The female probably differs as indicated for the preceding species. The birds of this genus are not well represented in the national collection, and but few examples are sexed.

GLAUCOUS MACAW (*Anodorhynchus glaucus*).

Only a male was sexed, but the probable female is slightly smaller, and has a shorter but equally broad beak, with a shorter but sharper terminal hook. In this example the throat is browner than in the sexed male, but whether this is a constant character I cannot say.

Spix's Macaw (*Cyanopsittacus spixi*).

Only a female is sexed, but the probable male has a broader and slightly larger beak, with a longer terminal hook ; it is also a larger bird.

Blue-and-Yellow Macaw (*Ara ararauna*).

The female is slightly smaller than the male; has a shorter, narrower beak, with shorter terminal hook.

Red-and-Blue Macaw (*Ara macao*).

Only the male is sexed. The probable female is smaller, with shorter but equally broad beak, and shorter terminal hook.

Red-and-Yellow Macaw (*Ara chloroptera*).

The sexes agree in size, but the male has a longer beak, narrower when viewed in profile ; the culmen less arched, the terminal hook variable in length, perhaps owing to wearing down through age.

Military Macaw (*Ara militaris*).

The male is slightly larger than the female, and has a distinctly longer beak, with less arched culmen; in young males the terminal hook is probably longer than in young females, but with advanced age it gets much worn down.

Severe Macaw (*Ara severa*).

Only the male is sexed in the Museum ; the probable female has a shorter beak, and more arched culmen.

Illiger's Macaw (*Ara maracana*).

The male is slightly the larger bird, and has a rather longer beak ; but the sexual differences are less strongly defined than usual.

Noble Macaw (*Ara nobilis*).

The male is larger than the female, his beak is rather longer, and a trifle fuller towards the terminal hook. As with the preceding species, the sexual differences are not so well marked as usual.

Hahn's Macaw (*Ara hahni*).

In this species the skull and beak of the male are narrower than in the female ; the beak also is longer, and though narrower at base, comparatively fuller before the commencement of the terminal hook.

We now come to the true Conures, of which Mr Seth-Smith says : "The sexes are, outwardly, alike in the Conures, although the males are slightly larger than the females " (*Parrakeets*, p. 27). These birds are numerous in species, and consequently the present chapter will be longer than usual.

SHARP-TAILED CONURE (*Conurus acuticaudatus*).

Contrary to what one would expect, the beak of the sexed female in the Museum series is distinctly narrower, both viewed from above and in profile, than that of the male; the terminal hook also is longer. This species therefore would seem to have the normal sexual characters reversed.

BLUE-CROWNED CONURE (*Conurus hæmorrhous*).

I found no sexed specimens; but as this species is nearly related to the preceding, it is not improbable that it possesses the same abnormal sexual peculiarities.

GOLDEN CONURE (*Conurus guarouba*).

In the sexed examples the male has a longer and less curved beak than the female; its plumage, as regards the yellow colouring of the body, is also brighter and more tinted with orange.

YELLOW CONURE (*Conurus solstitialis*).

The beak of the male is longer and rather broader than that of the female: it is also a trifle deeper when viewed in profile.

YELLOW-HEADED CONURE (*Conurus jendaya*).

I found no sexed specimens of this species, but it is pretty certain that the male will prove to have a longer and slightly broader beak than the female.

GOLDEN-HEADED CONURE (*Conurus auricapillus*).

The male has a longer and broader beak than the female; it is also deeper when viewed in profile.

BLACK-HEADED CONURE (*Conurus nanday*).

Although the beaks of the sexes are about equal in length, that of the male is distinctly broader than that of the female, and deeper when viewed in profile.

RED-MASKED CONURE (*Conurus rubrolarvatus*).

No sexed specimens, but it is highly probable that the male has a broader beak than the female.

WAGLER'S CONURE (*Conurus wagleri*).

As with the preceding, no specimens were sexed; it is probable that the male has the broader beak.

GREEN CONURE (*Conurus leucophthalmus*).

The beak of the male is narrower at the base, and has a more slender terminal hook than that of the female.

The Red-collared Conure (*C. rubritorquis*) is now considered to be a mere variety of the following :—

Mexican Conure (*Conurus holochlorus*).

In this species the beak of the male is narrower than that of the female.

Aztec Conure (*Conurus aztec*).

The beak of the male is slightly narrower at the base than that of the female, and the terminal hook is more slender.

Cactus Conure (*Conurus cactorum*).

The male is decidedly the larger bird, and has the longer beak.

Brown-throated Conure (*Conurus æruginosus*).

According to sexed specimens in the Natural History Museum, the male has a broader and shorter beak than the female. If the sexing of the various species of Conures is correct in every instance, and there is no reason why one should suppose that it is not, the structural peculiarities of the sexes seem to follow no definite rule in this group, the male sometimes having a long and narrow beak such as one would expect to find in that sex, and sometimes a broad and short beak such as one would expect to be characteristic of a female bird. It is, however, possible that some males are more active in the defence of their nests than others, and their weapons have been modified in consequence. In the sexed males of this species the cheeks and sides of throat are washed with greyish vinaceous, but the colouring of the species is variable.

St Thomas' Conure (*Conurus pertinax*).

Of this species I found no sexed specimens in the Museum; but what I take to be females have shorter and broader beaks than the others.

Golden-crowned Conure (*Conurus aureus*).

The female has a broader and shorter beak than the male.

Petz's Conure (*Conurus canicularis*).

The male has a much heavier and more curved beak than the female.

Carolina Conure (*Conuropsis carolinensis*).

In the male the beak is broader and very slightly longer than in the female.

Smaller Patagonian Conure (*Cyanolyseus patagonus*).

The female is smaller than the male; the beak is smaller, shorter, but broader at base.

Larger Patagonian Conure (*Cyanolyseus byroni*).

The male in the Museum sexed specimens is smaller than the female; the beak is longer, straighter, and more gradually tapered, with more slender terminal hook.

SLIGHT-BILLED PARRAKEET (*Henicognathus leptorhynchus*).

The beak of the male is generally broader than that of the female, though not at its base; it is distinctly longer.

CHILIAN CONURE (*Microsittace ferruginea*).

The male is larger than the female; its beak is slightly longer, broader, and more curved.

RED-EARED CONURE (*Pyrrhura cruentata*).

The male is the larger bird; its beak is narrower, slightly longer, more arched, not quite so deep at the base when viewed in profile.

RED-BELLIED CONURE (*Pyrrhura vittata*).

The male is slightly larger than the female; its beak is broader, longer, with more slender terminal hook.

WHITE-EARED CONURE (*Pyrrhura leucotis*).

The male is distinctly larger than the female; its beak is more slender, longer, less arched.

BLUE-WINGED CONURE (*Pyrrhura picta*).

The male is noticeably larger than his mate; its beak is broader at base, longer and more gradually tapered.

PEARLY CONURE (*Pyrrhura perlata*).

I could discover no sexed specimens, but, judging by their size, I believe the sexual differences are much the same as in *P. leucotis.*

QUAKER OR GREY-BREASTED PARRAKEET (*Myopsittacus monachus*).

A comparison of the sexed specimens in the Museum led me to the conclusion that the female of this species was much larger than the male, and has a considerably longer and more powerful beak. These differences do not strike one so much in the living specimens, but the female has a heavier appearance, even in a cage, and it is probable that, when my pair made their way from one aviary to another by clipping out a large circle in the dividing $\frac{1}{2}$-in. wire-netting, most of the work was done by the female. It requires a very powerful beak to cut netting of this size. It is probable that the hen cuts most of the sticks to form the remarkable nest made by this Parrakeet.

LINEOLATED PARRAKEET (*Bolborhynchus lineolatus*).

The female is smaller than the male, the beak very slightly different; but, judging by the sexed examples in the Museum, the plumage is not identical as stated, the rump being much less strongly spotted with black than the male, and the tail wholly green, the feathers not being broadly tipped with black as in the male.

PASSERINE OR BLUE-WINGED PARROTLET (*Psittacula passerina*).

The female is slightly smaller than the male; her beak is more arched and blunter; she shows no blue in her plumage, being wholly green, the rump being bright emerald green.

Of the species of the genus *Brotogerys*, Mr Seth-Smith says (*Parrakeets*, p. 78): "The sexes are outwardly alike, but the males are, as a rule, slightly larger than the females." In addition to this character, I find that there is always a difference in the outline of the beaks. One character noticeable in the males of some of the species is a slight angulation in the outline when viewed from above, owing to the fact that the extremity of the cutting-edge of the upper mandible projects outwards just in front of the terminal hook.

ALL-GREEN PARRAKEET (*Brotogerys tirica*).

The female is smaller than the male; her beak is shorter and much broader, more bell-shaped when viewed from above.

CANARY-WINGED PARRAKEET (*Brotogerys chiriri*).

The beak of the male is broader than that of the female, and shows a slight lateral angle at the end of the cutting-edge of the upper mandible when viewed from above.

WHITE-WINGED PARRAKEET (*Brotogerys virescens*).

This has been called "Yellow-winged," but the primaries are mostly white, and the secondaries white tinged with yellow. The beak of the male is more slender, and has a better-defined ridge (culmen); the angle at the end of the cutting-edge of the upper mandible is clearly visible from above.

ORANGE-FLANKED PARRAKEET (*Brotogerys pyrrhopterus*).

I could find no sexed specimens in the Museum series, but the smaller birds with shorter beaks are probably females.

TOVI PARRAKEET (*Brotogerys jugularis*).

In the male the beak is broader, longer, and less arched than in the female.

GOLDEN-FRONTED PARRAKEET (*Brotogerys tuipara*).

The beak of the male is shorter than that of the female, more arched, and when viewed from above shows a projecting angle at the end of the cutting-edge of the upper mandible.

GOLDEN-WINGED PARRAKEET (*Brotogerys chrysopterus*).

The beak of the male is broader at the base than in the female, and shows a more defined dorsal ridge; it is also shorter, and when seen from above shows an indication of a lateral angle as in *B. tuipara*.

TUI PARRAKEET (*Brotogerys tui*).

The male has a broader and longer beak than the female.

Owing to the fact that the *Conurinæ* exhibit no constant feature characteristic of sex, but each species has to be separately studied, it was not worth while to illustrate the sexual differences in any one species as a general guide to the student; it is enough to point out what differences exist in each species as evidence that in none of them is there any difficulty in discovering whether one has both sexes by carefully comparing the outline of the beaks from above and in profile.

CHAPTER XXIII.

AMAZONS, ETC. (*Pioninæ*).

I BELIEVE it is a general rule in the case of the Amazons for the eyes of the males to be darker than those of the females, but it is possible that in both sexes they may deepen somewhat with age, which would account for slight discrepancies which occur in descriptions of the same species, or such vague indications as one finds in some of Dr Russ' descriptions—"yellow to orange-red," though more probably in this case the "yellow" represents the iris of the female, the "orange-red" that of the male.

Count Salvadori usually speaks of the females as "like the male"; sometimes he adds, "perhaps a little duller," and in one or two instances he mentions a difference, but is uncertain whether it characterises a female or a young bird; all this is disconcerting. On the other hand, the late Mr Abrahams unhesitatingly pronounced my Yellow-fronted Amazon a female, judging by the colour of its eyes, and dissection after death proved the correctness of his decision.

An examination of the numerous specimens of Amazons in the National Collection shows that (as in the preceding groups) the outline of the beak, although differing a good deal in the opposite sexes, does not always differ in the same manner, but is modified presumably by the habits of each species; thus it is reasonable to suppose that if the male is more energetic than the female in excavating or enlarging the nesting-cavity, his beak will be constructed especially with an eye to strength, and will be broad, short, but with a strong, sharp, but curved terminal tooth; if, on the other hand, his energies are directed to defence rather than construction, a longer beak, with a nearly straight conical stabbing hook, is likely to be more serviceable; when the female chiefly prepares the nesting-cavity or is active in defending her nest, she naturally requires the same tools or weapons, and thus it comes about that in a few species the rostral features of the sexes appear to be reversed; generally, however, the longer beak is characteristic of the males.

GUILDING'S AMAZON (*Chrysotis guildingi*).

The beak of the male is much narrower than that of the female, the culmen more arched.

AUGUST AMAZON (*Chrysotis augusta*).

According to Count Salvadori, the female is "perhaps a little duller" than the male; in the Museum series I only found the female sexed; the beak, however, probably differs as in the preceding species.

VINACEOUS AMAZON (*Chrysotis vinacea*).

The male is larger than the female; her beak is broader, but more compressed from the nostrils outwards on each side of the culmen; the latter is also more arched.*

BLUE-FACED AMAZON (*Chrysotis versicolor*).

I only found females sexed, but in wild examples the differences would probably be characteristic of the genus, the male with longer beak. Oddly enough, the two sexed examples in the Museum, though both labelled as females, look much like opposite sexes. Can captivity have modified the normal character of the beak, or is the cage-bird wrongly sexed?

GUATEMALAN AMAZON (*Chrysotis guatemalæ*).

In this species the male has a narrower beak, especially at the base, than the female, and the terminal hook is more slender.

MEALY AMAZON (*Chrysotis farinosa*).

The beak of the male is slightly narrower at the base, shorter, and with broader terminal hook than that of the female; the sexed males in the Museum have a large patch of yellow and red on the crown, the sexed females barely a trace of yellow and no red, yet Count Salvadori seems to think that the few yellow feathers on the crown indicate younger birds. I can only say that, if this is the case, the female specimens show no other indications of youth.

MERCENARY AMAZON (*Chrysotis mercenaria*).

I only found sexed females, but the males probably differ as in the preceding species.

ORANGE-WINGED AMAZON (*Chrysotis amazonica*).

The beak of the male is longer, more tapering, and less arched than that of the female.

BLUE-FRONTED AMAZON (*Chrysotis æstiva*).

The beak of the male is longer and narrower at the base than that of the female.

* Female a little duller, bill less bright red.—*Wied.*

Yellow-shouldered Amazon (*Chrysotis ochroptera*).

Only sexed males are indicated in the Museum, but the differences are probably as in the preceding species.

Yellow-fronted Amazon (*Chrysotis ochrocephala*).

The beak of the male is broader, especially towards and beyond the middle, than that of the female when viewed from above. The sexed females show no yellow on the crown. As in the case of *C. farinosa*, Count Salvadori regards this character as an evidence of youth; but it is odd that this youthful feature should only occur in the specimens sexed as females, not in those sexed as males.

Yellow-billed Amazon (*Chrysotis panamensis*).

Only a male sexed. Probably it has a longer and narrower beak than the female, as in *C. amazonica*.

Golden-naped Amazon (*Chrysotis auripalliata*).

The beak of the male is broader than that of the female, more swollen just before the middle, less arched, and has a longer terminal hook.

Levaillant's Amazon (*Chrysotis levaillanti*).

The male is larger than the female, and his beak is slightly longer and rather narrower at the base when viewed from above.

Dufresne's Amazon (*Chrysotis dufresniana*).

The male is larger than the female, with decidedly longer and narrower beak.

Red-topped Amazon (*Chrysotis rhodocorytha*).

The male is larger and brighter in colour than the female; but, unlike the preceding species, his beak is shorter, broader, and more arched than hers.

Green-cheeked Amazon (*Chrysotis viridigena*).

The beaks of the sexes are much alike, but that of the male is a little heavier. The scarlet on the crown of the male extends farther backward than on that of the female.

Finsch's Amazon (*Chrysotis finschi*).

The male is larger than the female and a little brighter in plumage. The beak, as viewed from above, is narrower, slightly longer, with more slender terminal hook.

Diademed Amazon (*Chrysotis diademata*).

The National Collection at present only possesses one unsexed example; but it is probable that the beak of the male will prove to be longer than that of the female.

SALVIN'S AMAZON (*Chrysotis salvini*).

The male is larger and more brightly coloured than the female, and his beak is considerably longer, slightly broader, and less arched.

YELLOW-CHEEKED AMAZON (*Chrysotis autumnalis*).

The male is larger than the female, and the scarlet on his forehead broader; the female also shows less scarlet but more yellow on the cheeks. The beak of the male is much longer and heavier, with longer terminal hook.

RED-TAILED AMAZON (*Chrysotis braziliensis*).

Judging by the sexed specimens in the Museum, the male is larger than the female, much redder on the head, the cheeks much more purplish-blue; but, of course, the single female may be a variety. The beak of the male is narrower at the base, but fuller towards the tip, with a heavier terminal hook.

BODINUS' AMAZON (*Chrysotis bodini*).

Only the female is sexed, but what I take for the male is larger, shows more red on the front of the crown, more lilac on the nape, also a slightly longer and broader beak.

FESTIVE AMAZON (*Chrysotis festiva*).

The male is larger than the female, with a longer and more regularly tapering beak; the terminal hook is variable (probably owing to the different ages of the specimens), but is frequently broader.

RED-FRONTED AMAZON (*Chrysotis vittata*).

In the Museum only a male is sexed; but, after comparing the six specimens, I conclude that its beak is probably longer and more slender than that of the female.

PRETRE'S AMAZON (*Chrysotis prætrii*).

Only a male is sexed (not female, as noted in Catalogue); the beak is probably broader than in the female.

WHITE-BROWED AMAZON (*Chrysotis albifrons*).*

The male has a longer beak, with a longer and more slender terminal hook.

YELLOW-LORED AMAZON (*Chrysotis xantholora*).

The beak of the male is more pointed towards the tip, the terminal hook being longer. In the only sexed female in the Museum series the crown is mostly blue, the forehead only being white; it

---

* In the Museum Catalogue, Count Salvadori says of this species (vol. xx. p. 312): "*Young or Female.*—Differs from the adult male in having the bastard-wing and primary coverts green, with no red."

also shows much less crimson round the eyes than the sexed males. Count Salvadori nevertheless says: "*Adult female.*—Apparently like the male." It must therefore be concluded that he regards the only sexed female as abnormal in colouring; yet it would not be extraordinary for the female to approach the young in colouring; and of the latter he says: "Sinciput blue, with no white; lores yellow, with some green scattered feathers; periophthalmic region and cubital edge green, with a few scattered red feathers," etc. Does the Count, perhaps, consider the only sexed female to be a young bird? If so, why does he note it afterwards as adult?

It appears to me that in many species of Parrots there seems to be a doubt in the mind of the cataloguer as to whether the birds are adult females or young birds; the female is generally smaller than the male, and more often than not has a broader and shorter beak; the young bird is, of course, smaller than either parent, and has a much broader beak than if he were adult. I think, nevertheless, by taking the largest sexed birds for comparison, one is likely to get the difference between adult sexes, and whenever possible I have adopted this plan.

Salle's Amazon (*Chrysotis ventralis*).

Only females are sexed in the Museum series. The probable male has a larger beak, slightly wider than in the females, and with very slightly longer terminal hook.

White-fronted Amazon (*Chrysotis leucocephala*).

Only the male is sexed in the Museum. The probable female is smaller, with much smaller and weaker beak; its crown is creamy white without a trace of rose-red. Count Salvadori seems to consider the latter as the typical form of the species, and the rose-flecked form as representing a common variety; but why should not the latter be the ordinary male? I found no sexed males without the rose colouring on the crown.

Bahamas' Amazon (*Chrysotis bahamensis*).

Not represented in the National Collection; but I saw a beautiful pair in one of my friend Mr J. L. Bonhote's aviaries, and the male appeared to me to have a longer and less arched beak than the female; but, although invited to do so by the owner, I did not feel tempted to handle the birds in order to ascertain their exact sexual differences.

Red-throated Amazon (*Chrysotis collaria*).

The beak of the male is more slender and has a longer terminal hook than that of the female. The only sexed female shows much less white on the crown than the males. One of the latter is evidently a young bird, if it is correctly sexed, as it is a small specimen with rather a heavy beak.

ACTIVE AMAZON (*Chrysotis agilis*).

The beak of the male is longer and slightly narrower than that of the female, and has a longer terminal hook.

SHORT-TAILED PARROT (*Pachynus brachyurus*).

The beak of the male is shorter and heavier than that of the female, and has a broader terminal hook. In the sexed example of the female the naked skin round the eye is much darker than in the male. The structure of the beak in this species is interesting as being a reversal of the usual sexual differences in the true Amazons.

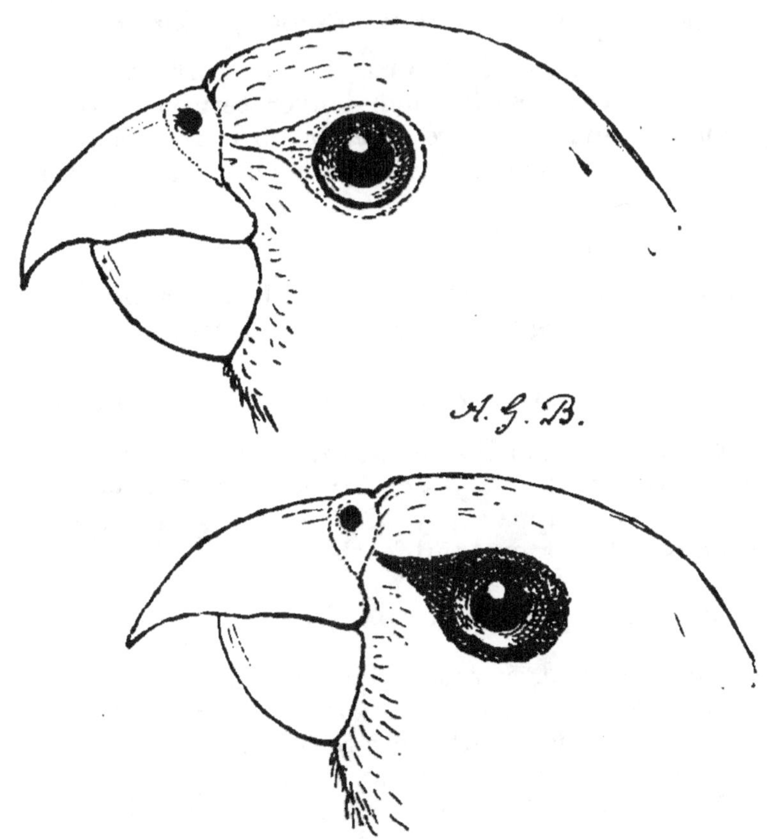

HEADS OF MALE AND FEMALE SHORT-TAILED PARROT.

RED-VENTED PARROT (*Pionus menstruus*).

As in the preceding species, the beak of the male in this Parrot is larger and broader than that of the female, with a shorter terminal hook.

SORDID PARROT (*Pionus sordidus*).

Only the male is sexed in the Museum. The female is probably a smaller bird, having a rather broader beak; but, unhappily, there are only three examples in the National Collection.

MAXIMILIAN'S PARROT (*Pionus maximiliani*).

In fully adult males the beak is much larger, though rather more slender than that of the females ; but in young birds (as might have been expected) the beak is almost as broad, excepting towards the tip, as that of the female.

WHITE-HEADED PARROT (*Pionus senilis*).

In this species the beak of the male is larger, longer, and less arched than that of the female, the terminal hook is also longer, and the entire bird slightly larger.

BRONZE-WINGED PARROT (*Pionus chalcopterus*).

If one compares fully adult birds, the male of this species has a far more slender beak, with much longer terminal hook, than the female ; younger and therefore smaller birds are much more alike, the beaks of the males being then of a much more feminine type.

DUSKY PARROT (*Pionus fuscus*).

The male is larger than the female. It has a larger and more slender beak, with a slightly longer terminal hook.

HAWK-HEADED CAIQUE (*Deroptyus accipitrinus*).

The male is larger than the female, its beak is altogether heavier. Count Salvadori says (*Catalogue of Birds*, vol. xx. p. 337) : "*Female.* —Like the male, but apparently with no red spots at the bases of the inner webs of the lateral tail-feathers."

RED-CAPPED PARROT (*Pionopsittacus pileatus*).

In the male the beak is rather larger and narrower than in the female. Count Salvadori says (*Catalogue of Birds*, vol. xx. p. 341) : "*Female.*—Like the male, but the forehead tinged with blue, no red whatever on the pileum ; crown and occiput green with an olive tinge." There is one example sexed as a female which is coloured like the males, so we must conclude that the Count decided this sexing to be incorrect.

BLACK-HEADED CAIQUE (*Caica melanocephala*).

When viewed from above the beak of the male is seen to be broader and a trifle shorter than that of the female.

WHITE-BELLIED CAIQUE (*Caica leucogaster*).

Only a male is sexed, and Count Salvadori does not mention the female. It is probable that the sexes differ as in the preceding species.

YELLOW-THIGHED CAIQUE (*Caica xanthomera*).

Only a female is sexed.   It probably differs from the male as in the allied species.

We now come to some African Parrots, which (although referred to the *Pioninæ*) would, I think, be more conveniently placed with the few other African forms of the subfamily *Psittacinæ*.   I shall therefore commence Chapter XXIV. with these; not, of course, transferring them to the next subfamily, but merely placing them in the same chapter with them.

CHAPTER XXIV.

AFRICAN PIONINÆ.

LEVAILLANT'S PARROT (*Pæocephalus robustus*).

THE beak of the male is slightly narrower and considerably longer than that of the female, and in the Museum examples the terminal hook is far more acute.

BROWN-NECKED PARROT (*Pæocephalus fuscicollis*).

Only a male is sexed in the Museum series, but it probably has a longer beak, with longer terminal hook, than the female.

JARDINE'S PARROT (*Pæocephalus gulielmi*).

The male is larger than the female, and has a considerably heavier and more powerful beak.

BROWN-HEADED PARROT (*Pæocephalus fuscicapillus*).

The male is larger than the female, but the beak exhibits little, if any, structural difference.

SENEGAL PARROT.
(*From a Photograph by Miss Alderson.*)

SENEGAL PARROT (*Pæocephalus senegalus*).

No specimens are sexed in the Museum, but the male is probably larger than the female, with a rather heavier beak.

MEYER'S PARROT (*Pæocephalus meyeri*).

The male is larger than the female, and his beak is much more powerful, with a longer terminal hook.

RUEPPELL'S PARROT (*Præocephalus rueppelli*).

The male has a more powerful beak than the female; but the latter, as pointed out by Count Salvadori, is by far the more showy bird, the lower back, rump, and upper tail-coverts being bright blue. It also differs in the paler blue wash on the vent and under tail-coverts (see *Catalogue of Birds*, vol. xx. p. 376). If there is any blue in the males, it is very inconspicuous.

Typical Parrots (*Psittacinæ*).

GREY PARROT (*Psittacus erythrura*).

I am afraid my drawing [The drawing Dr Butler alludes to appeared in No. 1 of *Canary and Cage-Bird Life*, together with a long article on the Grey Parrot.—ED.] of the heads of this species is a little faulty as regards the beak of the male, which should be longer than that of the female. When viewed from above, it is also fuller just before the terminal hook. In addition to these characters, the naked patch enclosing the eye is much more rounded at the back in the hen than in the cock, and (as a general rule) the hen is a darker bird, but the plumage of this species varies a good deal.

TIMNEH PARROT (*Psittacus timneh*).

This appears to me to be no more than a race of the Grey Parrot. The male is larger than the female, and his beak is decidedly longer and rather fuller before the terminal hook, when seen from above. The other characters also hold good.

GREATER VASA PARROT (*Coracopsis vasa*).

In the Museum series only one male is sexed; the female is probably smaller, with a shorter and less powerful beak. Such is notably the case with an immature bird in the series.*

LESSER VASA PARROT (*Coracopsis nigra*).

Only a male is sexed; the probable female is smaller, with a shorter and slightly weaker beak. It is probable that Count Salvadori also considered the same specimen to be the female, as he states that the female is "smaller."

PRASLIN PARROT (*Coracopsis barklyi*).

The sexed female is palpably smaller than the male, and has a smaller, weaker beak.

We now come to the *Palæornithinæ*, a fairly large group of handsome birds, in which the sexes are generally easy to distinguish by plumage alone. I have nevertheless gone carefully over them,

---

* "*Female*.—Duller" (Salvadori, *Catalogue of Birds*, vol. xx. p. 382).

comparing the structural differences in their beaks, which in fully adult specimens are frequently noteworthy. Of course, it must always be borne in mind that young examples still show the broad nestling type of beak, which more frequently than not is characteristic in a more or less modified condition of female birds, though in some cases habits of the particular species have rendered it characteristic of the males, as I have already pointed out.

MRS GRIFFIN'S GREY PARROT.
(*From a Photograph by Mr W. H. Hall, Widnes.*)

CHAPTER XXV.

RING-NECKS AND ALLIES (*Palæornithinæ*).

RED-SIDED ECLECTUS (*Eclectus pectoralis*).

IN addition to the startling differences of plumage in the sexes—the prevalence of bright green in the male and scarlet in the female, the red iris of the male and the yellow one in the female, the red upper mandible of the male and the wholly black beak of the female —the male beak is much longer and fuller in front of the terminal hook than that of the female.

GRAND ECLECTUS (*Eclectus roratus*).

The male of this species is very similar to that of the preceding bird, but the green colouring is a trifle more yellow, the lateral tail-feathers usually bluer, and the upper mandible is tipped with yellow. The female is thus described: "Red, the head brighter; collar round the nape covering the upper back, lower breast, and abdomen purple; the upper breast red, tinged with purple; under tail-coverts and a band at the tip of the tail, bright yellow; primaries and their wing-coverts, deep blue; secondaries, red on the outer web, blue at the tip and on the inner web; the innermost secondaries, near the scapulars, entirely red; tail, underneath, golden red, towards the base dusky; iris yellow; bill and feet, black" (Salvadori, in *Catalogue of Birds*, vol. xx. p. 394). The measurements given show that the male is the larger bird; his beak is much broader, more powerful, and the culmen is less arched than that of the female.

WESTERMANN'S ECLECTUS (*Eclectus Westermanni*).

Unhappily the female of this species is not known at present. No doubt the male will prove to possess a more powerful beak.

In the species of *Tanygnathus* the sexes are much alike in plumage, but the female is generally smaller than the male.

BLUE-CROWNED PARRAKEET (*Tanygnathus luconensis*).

Apart from its superior size, the male can be distinguished from the female by its altogether longer, larger, and more powerful beak.

GREAT-BILLED PARRAKEET (*Tanygnathus megalorhynchus*).

Count Salvadori actually notes the smaller size of the beak in the female of this species, and Mr Seth-Smith says that the female is smaller than the male. When viewed from above, the beak of the male is noticeably broader than that of the female.

MUELLER'S PARRAKEET (*Tanygnathus muelleri*).

The beak of the male is slightly longer, more arched, and fuller just before the commencement of the terminal hook when viewed from above.

The sexes of many of the species of *Palæornis* are distinguishable by plumage alone, but in fully adult birds the sexual differences in the form of the beak are always noticeable. The females are generally smaller than the males. In the forms of Alexandrine Parrakeets, in addition to their superior size, the males have a more arched and slightly narrower beak than the females; this last character is especially noticeable just before the base of the terminal hook.

CINGHALESE ALEXANDRINE PARRAKEET (*Palæornis eupatria*).

"The female lacks the black stripes on the neck and the rose collar, and is slightly smaller than the male" (Seth-Smith, *Parrakeets*, p. 97).

NEPALESE ALEXANDRINE PARRAKEET (*Palæornis nepalensis*).

"The female lacks the black stripes and rose collar" (Seth-Smith, *l. c.*, p. 99).

INDO-BURMESE ALEXANDRINE PARRAKEET (*Palæornis indoburmana*).

The female lacks the black mandibular stripes and rose collar, according to Salvadori.

GREAT-BILLED ALEXANDRINE PARRAKEET (*Palæornis magnirostris*).

The female, as usual, "differs from the male, wanting the black mandibular stripes and the red collar. Size rather smaller" (Salvadori, *Catalogue of Birds*, vol. xx. p. 441).

MAURITIAN RING-NECKED PARRAKEET (*Palæornis eques*).

"*Female.*—Differs from the male in having no bluish tinge on the occiput, no rose collar, and no black mandibular stripes, there being only a trace of the latter of a dark green colour; . . . bill entirely dusky black. Dimensions as in the male, but the bill a little smaller" (Salvadori, *Catalogue of Birds*, vol. xx. p. 443).

INDIAN RING-NECKED PARRAKEET (*Palæornis torquata*).

In fully adult birds the beak of the male is braoder at the base and more regularly triangular when viewed from above than that of the female. In a smaller and evidently young female in the Museum the beak is more nearly of the male type. "*Female.*—

Wants the black loral line, and also the black and rose collars and the black mandibular stripes; an indistinct collar of emerald green round the neck. Size a little smaller than the male" (Salvadori, *Catalogue of Birds*, vol. xx. p. 445).

African Ring-necked Parrakeet (*Palæornis docilis*).

In adult birds the beak of the male is shorter, broader before the terminal hook, the latter being a little smaller than in the female. Young females more nearly resemble the male in these characters. In plumage the sexes differ much as in the preceding species.

Blossom-headed Parrakeet (*Palæornis cyanocephala*)

The male is larger than the female; the beak rather more curved, forming a more regular triangle when viewed from above, that of the female being fuller in the middle. In the latter sex the colouring is very different; "the head dull plum-blue, more greyish on the forehead and cheeks; a yellow collar, broader on the sides of the neck; no black collar and no black mandibular stripes; no red patch on the median upper wing-coverts. Upper mandible yellow, lower dusky or blackish" (Salvadori, *Catalogue of Birds*, vol. xx. p. 451).

Rosy-headed or Rosa's Parrakeet (*Palæornis rosa*).

Male larger than female, with broader, deeper, and generally more powerful beak. "The female may readily be distinguished from the female of *P. cyanocephala* by the *red spot on the wing-coverts* being present as in the male. The head is more greyish, and the yellow collar less distinct" (Seth-Smith, *Parrakeets*, p. 107).

Slaty-headed Parrakeet (*Palæornis schisticeps*).

Of this rarely imported species Mr Seth-Smith says: "The female lacks the red wing-patch, but is otherwise like the male" (*Parrakeets*, p. 108). The same is true of the Burmese Slaty-headed Parrakeet (*Palæornis finschi*), another very rarely imported species.

Malabar Parrakeet (*Palæornis peristerodes*).

I failed to find this species in the Museum owing to it standing under the hybrid Latin and Greek name of *columboïdes*. Mr Seth-Smith says of it: "The female, which is slightly smaller than the male, lacks the green forehead and the bluish-green collar, and has a blackish bill" (*Parrakeets*, p. 110).

Derbyan Parrakeet (*Palæornis derbyana*).

A very rare species not in the Museum. As regards sexual differences, Mr Seth-Smith says: "The male has the upper mandible red, whereas in the female both mandibles are black" (*Parrakeets*, p. 112).

Banded or Moustache Parrakeet (*Palæornis fasciata*).

The beak of the male is broader and more powerful than that of the female, of which Count Salvadori writes: "Differs in having the head tinged with blue, and the vinaceous red of the breast produced up the sides of the neck between the lilac-blue of the head and the emerald green of the neck; bill black, with the base of the lower mandible orange-brown" (*Catalogue of Birds*, vol. xx. p. 466). Oddly enough, one of the specimens from the Hume series in the Museum, which in size, colouring, and everything else would seem to be a female, shows a considerable amount of red on the beak. Is this, perhaps, the first stage in the assumption of male plumage by an old female?

Blyth's Nicobar Parrakeet (*Palæornis caniceps*).

Extremely rare as a captive bird. The female may be distinguished, as Count Salvadori tells us, by "the grey colour of the pileum and nape (being) tinged with bluish; the bill wholly black" (*Catalogue of Birds*, vol. xx. p. 470).

Lucian Parrakeet (*Palæornis modesta*).

The male is larger than the female; the beak slightly longer, more arched, not so full towards the terminal hook. "The female has the top of the head greenish-brown; the stripes, which are black in the male, are dark bluish-green, almost black, in the female; cheeks and ear-coverts reddish, the latter edged behind with a bluish band" (Seth-Smith, *Parrakeets*, p. 117).

Nicobar Parrakeet (*Palæornis nicobarica*).

The male is larger than the female; his beak is a little longer, and generally more powerful. "The female has both mandibles blackish, and the red colour of the cheeks duller" (*Parrakeets*, p. 118).

Although probable, it is not certain that the Andaman Parrakeet has been imported, so I need not consider it here.

Long-tailed Parrakeet (*Palæornis longicauda*).

In the males the beak is broader at base and more triangular when viewed from above than in the females; the terminal hook is also longer. In the female the entire beak is horny brown, and the mandibular stripes are dark green instead of black.

Barraband's Parrakeet (*Polytelis barrabandi*)

The male is scarcely larger than the female; but his beak is more arched, broader, and deeper, with shorter terminal hook. "The female is much duller green; the throat and upper breast greyish-rose; thighs scarlet; inner webs of tail-feathers rose-pink" (Seth-Smith, *Parrakeets*, p. 122).

BLACK-TAILED PARRAKEET (*Polytelis melanura*).

The beak of the male is of a brighter red than that of the female; it is shorter and more arched, more triangular when viewed from above, with shorter terminal hook. "The female is dull olive-green, darker on the back; rump, breast, and abdomen olive, with a yellowish tinge; a greenish-yellow patch on the wing-coverts; quills deep blue; some red on the secondaries and greater wing-coverts; tail-feathers bluish-green, the lateral ones margined on the inner webs, and tipped with rose" (*Parrakeets*, p. 124).

ALEXANDRA PARRAKEET (*Spathopterus alexandræ*).

The beak of the male is of a brighter red than that of the female; it is distinctly broader and more arched; he is also a larger bird, has a bluer crown, greener cheeks and under parts, especially as regards the breast. He also possesses spatular terminations to the third primary, which are wanting in the female. It is on this character that the genus *Spathopterus* has been based, and, therefore, according to some modern workers, who ignore secondary sexual characters, it would be regarded as a mere section of the genus *Polytelis*.

CRIMSON-WINGED PARRAKEET (*Ptistes erythropterus*).

The male is larger than the female, and his beak is much shorter, more arched, and more triangular when viewed from above. "The adult female is dull green, more yellowish below; rump blue; some of the upper wing-coverts tipped with red; the lateral tail-feathers edged with pink on the inner webs" (Seth-Smith, *Parrakeets*, p. 131).

KING PARRAKEET (*Aprosmictus cyanopygius*).

The beak of the male is considerably longer, more arched, and with much longer terminal hook than that of the female. "The adult female has the head, back, wings, and tail dark green; throat and chest duller green, with a vinous tinge; abdomen and flanks scarlet; bill blackish" (*Parrakeets*, p. 134).

RED-SHINING PARRAKEET (*Pyrrhulopsis splendens*).

The male is larger than the female; his beak is altogether larger, longer, more arched, with more slender terminal hook. The plumage does not differ in the sexes.

TABUAN PARRAKEET (*Pyrrhulopsis tabuensis*).

The male is larger than the female; his beak is much longer, with longer terminal hook. The plumage of the sexes is similar.

MASKED PARRAKEET (*Pyrrhulopsis personata*).

The male is larger than the female, and has a longer, broader, and altogether much heavier beak. In the colouring of their plumage both sexes are alike.

THE MASKED PARRAKEET.
(From a Photograph by Miss Alderson.)

BLUE-RUMPED PARRAKEET
(*Psittinus incertus*).

The beak of the male is decidedly longer than that of the female. When viewed from above, it is elongate-conical, whereas that of the female would be better described as triangular in outline. "The female has the head and nape reddish-brown, the sides of the head with a yellowish tinge, the shafts being dusky; back and upper tail-coverts green; a small patch of blue on the lower back; the under parts yellowish - green, the breast feathers being darker in the centre, producing a scaly appearance" (Seth-Smith, *Parrakeets*, page 139).

MADAGASCAR LOVE-BIRD (*Agapornis cana*).

The male has a rather narrower beak than the female. She also differs in wanting the ashy grey on head and breast and the black on under wing-coverts. In fact, excepting for the black and yellowish on the tail-feathers, her plumage is practically uniform green.

RED-FACED LOVE-BIRD (*Agapornis pullaria*).

The male is larger than the female, his beak is longer, less arched, with longer terminal hook. The female, also, as in the preceding species, has green under wing-coverts (whereas the male has black); her beak is less bright in colour, and her face and rump paler.

ROSY OR PEACH-FACED LOVE-BIRD (*Agapornis roseicollis*).

The male is rather larger than the female; his beak is longer, less arched; when viewed from above it forms an elongate cone, whereas that of the female is distinctly less elongate. In this sex, also, the rosy colouring on the breast is noticeably more restricted than in the male.

VERNAL HANGING PARRAKEET (*Loriculus vernalis*).

"In the female the green colour is rather more yellowish, and the head less brilliant green; blue of the throat almost or entirely absent" (Seth-Smith, *Parrakeets*, p. 153).

GOLDEN-BACKED HANGING PARRAKEET (*Loriculus chrysonotus*).

The male is slightly larger than the female; his beak is shorter, less arched, slightly narrower at base. "The female has the cheeks and throat tinged with blue; throat with *no red patch;* back green, washed with golden; the golden colour on the head and nape less bright than in the male" (*Parrakeets*, p. 154).

CEYLONESE HANGING PARRAKEET (*Loriculus indicus*).

The male is larger than the female; his beak is much longer, less arched, narrower at base; the plumage of the sexes is similar.

BLUE-CROWNED HANGING PARRAKEET (*Loriculus galgulus*).

The beak of the male is narrower, slightly longer and less arched than that of the female. The latter sex is distinctly duller in all its colours, has no crimson on the throat or yellow belt across the lower back.

SCLATER'S HANGING PARRAKEET (*Loriculus sclateri*).

No specimens bore sex marks in the Museum, and the colouring appeared to be very variable; but what seemed most likely to be the males show a broader crimson patch on the throat, and have a more arched beak, whereas in the others the crimson on the throat is represented by a more or less narrow crimson or orange-red longitudinal streak. The question is: Are these differences sexual, or dependent upon age? Count Salvadori says: "*Female.—*Like the male."

CHAPTER XXVI.

BROADTAILS, ETC. (*Platycercinæ*).

THE Zoological Society uses the term "Broadtails" for this sub-family, and I have followed their lead in the second part of *Foreign Bird-Keeping;* but Dr Sharpe objects to the term as confusing when applied to Parrakeets, inasmuch as it has also been used for an entirely unrelated group of birds. In like manner one might equally object to the term "Manakin" in use among ornithologists for a group in no way related to the Finches known as Mannikins. At the same time I think it will simplify matters to speak of these Broadtails as "Parrakeets," as has been done in Mr Seth-Smith's admirable work.

PENNANT'S PARRAKEET (*Platycercus elegans*).

The male is altogether brighter than the female, and shows less green in the tail; the beak when viewed from above is noticeably fuller at the middle.   The very rare Masters' Parrakeet probably differs in much the same way.

ADELAIDE PARRAKEET (*Platycercus Adelaidæ*).

The male is brighter in colouring, more distinctly marked, and its tail is less green than that of the female.   His beak, seen from above, is generally fuller, and much broader at the base.

YELLOW-RUMPED PARRAKEET (*Platycercus flaveolus*).

Only the male is sexed in the Museum series, but, judging from the form of its beak, it should differ from the female in the same manner as *P. elegans*.

YELLOW-BELLIED PARRAKEET (*Platycercus flaviventris*).

The male is brighter than the female, not generally so green; its beak is altogether fuller when viewed from above.

MEALY OR PALE-HEADED ROSELLA (*Platycercus pallidiceps*).

I found no sexed specimens in the Museum, but what I take to be the male is larger, altogether more brightly coloured, and has a fuller beak when seen from above than what is presumably the female.

BLUE-CHEEKED PARRAKEET (*Platycercus amathusia*).

Only one male in poor condition sexed.   So far as I could judge, it would seem to differ from the female in its fuller beak.

BROWN'S PARRAKEET (*Platycercus browni*).

No examples were sexed in the Collection, but the sexes probably differ as in other species of the genus.

The Red-mantled Parrakeet (*Platycercus erythropeplus*) is now known to be only a hybrid between Pennant's Parrakeet and the common Rosella.

ROSELLA OR ROSE-HILL PARRAKEET (*Platycercus eximius*).

The male is brighter in colour, larger, its beak longer and a little broader at base than in the female.   The late Mr Abrahams on one occasion called my attention to a pair of these birds, and asked me if I could see a difference in marking between them.   After careful examination I said that the only difference I could discover was that one had a small round green spot on the crimson of the nape, which was wanting in the other.   "Exactly," replied Mr Abrahams; "that is an invariable character of the female."   Subsequently, on talking it over with Mr Camps, the well-known judge of these birds, he expressed doubt of the validity of this character, saying that the colouring of the nape was very variable.   A study of the skins in the Museum justifies the latter statement, one sexed male showing a large patch of green on the nape; but, at the same time, it is a significant fact that the only specimen in which there is a small rounded green spot on the red is the only one sexed as a female.

YELLOW-MANTLED PARRAKEET (*Platycercus splendidus*).

This rarely imported species probably differs in the same way as the other species—in the fuller beak of the male when viewed from above.

STANLEY PARRAKEET (*Platycercus icterotis*).

No examples in the Collection were sexed, but, so far as I could judge, the male shows less green in the plumage than the female, and has a heavier beak.

PILEATED PARRAKEET (*Porphyrocephalus spurius*).

No specimens were sexed, but the more brightly coloured examples possess the heavier beaks, and Count Salvadori says that the female is " duller and smaller."

BARNARD'S PARRAKEET (*Barnardius barnardi*).

The male is larger than the female, brighter in colour, and possesses a longer and more powerful beak. Count Salvadori says (*Catalogue of Birds*, vol. xx. p. 559): " *Female.*—Like the male, only smaller and duller; the back less bluish and more greenish."

BAUER'S PARRAKEET (*Barnardius zonarius*).

I found no sexed specimens, but the probable male is brighter than the presumed female, has a blacker head, the beak less swollen at middle, more regularly triangular, wider towards tip.

YELLOW-NAPED PARRAKEET (*Barnardius semitorquatus*).

Count Salvadori simply describes the female as "smaller and duller than the male." A comparison of the sexes shows that its head is browner, and the green of its plumage decidedly deeper. Its beak is much shorter, and slightly broader at the base.

RED-VENTED BLUE-BONNET PARRAKEET (*Psephotus hœmatorrhous*).

No specimens were sexed, but I regard the two last enumerated in the Catalogue as representing the female; their beaks are altogether smaller and shorter than in the other examples.

YELLOW-VENTED BLUE-BONNET PARRAKEET (*Psephotus xanthorrhous*).

Sexes not indicated in the Museum, but they probably differ as in the preceding species, the female having a smaller beak than the male.

Beautiful Parrakeet (*Psephotus pulcherrimus*).

Only one female is sexed in the Museum; at anyrate, I failed to discover the male noted in the Catalogue (the sexed female is not noted). The female is altogether considerably less brightly coloured than the male, with little or no red on the forehead, less on the wing-coverts, abdomen and vent; all the bright golden green in the plumage is replaced by pale brassy yellowish, flecked or barred with golden ochre or red. According to Ramsay, the female is like the young male, and Count Salvadori describes the latter as follows :— " Forehead yellowish-grey, stained with red; sides of the head and back and breast greyish, stained with greenish; flanks, abdomen, and under tail-coverts pale blue, middle of the abdomen stained with red; wing-coverts greyish, stained with red; rump, upper tail-coverts, and tail as in the adult bird; quills with a white oblique band on the under surface" (*Catalogue of Birds*, vol. xx. p. 565).

Golden-shouldered Parrakeet (*Psephotus chrysopterygius*).

Mr Seth-Smith thus distinguishes the. female : "The female has the frontal band yellowish-white; crown brownish; sides of the head nearly white, washed with blue; under parts greenish, washed with blue down to the lower abdomen and under tail-coverts, which are marked with red and white, as in the male, but much fainter; back, scapulars, and upper wing-coverts yellowish-green, the yellow becoming brighter on the wing-patch; rump and upper tail-coverts bright blue; primaries blackish, edged with blue on the outer web; tail as in the male" (*Parrakeets*, p. 206). [This book can be had from this office for 40s.—Ed.]

Many-coloured Parrakeet (*Psephotus multicolor*).

The female is smaller than the male, with much shorter beak; she is altogether duller in colour; the frontal blue band is paler, as also the blue on the shoulder of the wing and the yellow on the under tail-coverts; there is less red on the abdomen. Mr Seth-Smith also lays emphasis on the red patch on the wing-coverts. He says : "The female is very different from the male, having the upper parts mostly brownish-grey, with an olive-green tinge; *patch on the wing-coverts red ;* frontal band reddish in some individuals, yellowish in others; some specimens have a faint patch of reddish on the occiput, which is absent in others; lower breast, abdomen, and under tail-coverts yellowish-green, with a bluish tinge; a faint indication of red on some of the feathers of the abdomen; rump, upper tail-coverts, and tail as in the male" (*Parrakeets*, pp. 210, 211).

Red-rumped Parrakeet (*Psephotus hœmatonotus*).

A female according to the sex-mark on its label appears to me to answer to Count Salvadori's description of the young bird. The beak is smaller and shorter than in the male; its head and shoulders are greyish-olive; there is little or no red on the rump, and no yellow or green on the under parts; this does not quite correspond with Mr Seth-Smith's description, in which we read: "Abdomen pale yellow; vent and under tail-coverts white; wing-coverts greyish-green, tinged with blue; primary-coverts and outer web of primaries dull blue," but it is possible that the example may be abnormal. The description in *Parrakeets* is sure to be reliable. The odd thing is that Salvadori, describing the young, says: "Middle of the abdomen yellow," yet my note was made from a Museum example marked as a female, and which, therefore, should have shown a yellow abdomen. Perhaps the light was not good, and my sight a little defective from ill-health.

Bourke's Parrakeet (*Neophema bourkei*).

The female is rather smaller than the male, has a much shorter beak, with thicker and less pointed terminal hook (but this last characteristic may vary with age); she is also "duller and paler; the blue frontal band wanting" (Salvadori).

Blue-winged Grass Parrakeet (*Neophema venusta*).

A rarely imported species, the female of which differs from the male in its duller colouring.

Elegant Grass Parrakeet (*Neophema elegans*).

The female is smaller than the male, as usual, with a considerably shorter beak; she is duller in colour, and has a narrower frontal blue band.

Orange-bellied Grass Parrakeet (*Neophema chrysogastra*).

The female of this rarely imported species is smaller and "duller than the male; the abdominal orange spot neither so extensive nor so brilliant" (Salvadori; *c.f.* Gould, *Handbook of Birds of Australia,* ii. p. 76, 1865).*

Turquoisine Grass Parrakeet (*Neophema pulchella*).

The female is smaller than the male, has a thicker, shorter beak, but differs as follows: "Above duller green; frontal band blue passing over and behind the eyes; a line before the blue frontal band, and lores pale yellowish; cheeks, tinged with blue; wings as in the male, only duller, and with no red-chestnut spot on the inner upper wing-coverts; throat and breast yellowish-green; tail as in the male" (Salvadori, *Catalogue of Birds,* vol. xx. p. 576).

Splendid Grass Parrakeet (*Neophema splendida*).

In the sexes of this species the beak differs very little, that of the female is perhaps a trifle broader; fortunately she differs a good deal in colour. "Much duller than the male; face and upper wing-

---

* There are no sexed specimens in the Museum, but what I take to be the female has a shorter beak with less acute terminal hook: it is not only much duller and with more restricted orange patch on the abdomen than the probable males, but its wings are much less blue.

coverts pale lazuline blue; no yellowish tinge on the lores as in the female of *N. pulchella*; no scarlet colour on the chest, which is green; upper parts, including the nape and crown, green with orange tinge" (Salvadori, *Catalogue of Birds*, vol. xx. p. 577).

ANTIPODES ISLAND PARRAKEET (*Cyanorhamphus unicolor*).

"*Female.*—Of smaller size and paler plumage that the male; bill greyish-white, the upper mandible brownish-black in its apical portion, and with a clouded bluish spot in front of each nostril" (Salvadori, *Catalogue of Birds*, vol. xx. p. 581).

NEW ZEALAND PARRAKEET (*Cyanorhamphus novæ-zealandiæ*).

"*Adult Female.*—Like the male, only smaller, and the frontal red cap not so conspicuous" (Salvadori, *Catalogue of Birds*, vol. xx. p. 583).

SAISSET'S PARRAKEET (*Cyanorhamphus saisseti*).

A rarely imported local race of the preceding. The female is smaller than the male.

GOLDEN-CROWNED PARRAKEET (*Cyanorhamphus auriceps*).

The sexes are much alike, but the female is smaller than the male.

ALPINE PARRAKEET (*Cyanorhamphus malherbei*).

No sexed examples in the Museum, but it is probable that the female is smaller that the male.

HORNED PARRAKEET (*Nymphicus cornutus*).

The male is larger and brighter in colouring than the female; his beak is rather broader and more regularly tapered.

UVÆAN PARRAKEET (*Nymphicus uvæensis*).

The male is altogether a trifle brighter in colouring than the female; his beak is much heavier, particularly towards the tip, and distinctly longer.

SWIFT PARRAKEET (*Nanodes discolor*).

The female is smaller and duller than the male. Her beak is rather narrower, but with broader and shorter terminal hook.

BUDGERIGAR (*Melopsittacus undulatus*).

The beak of the male is very slightly longer than that of the female; the cere is bright turquoise blue, whereas in the female it is pale blue with whitish borders, changing in the breeding season to coffee-brown. The plumage of the sexes is much alike, but the under parts of the male are perhaps of a rather bluer-green, especially on the under tail-coverts, than in the female, the yellow of the throat and sides of head a shade deeper, and the black barring more distinct.

Ground or Swamp Parrakeet (*Pezoporus terrestris*).

The female is slightly smaller than the male, and has a much smaller beak; she is duller in plumage, and has a narrower and duller frontal band.   The species is very rarely imported.

Night Parrakeet (*Geopsittacus occidentalis*).

The Museum specimens are not sexed, but it is probable that the male has a stronger beak than the female.

Night Parrot (*Stringops habroptilus*).

Only a male is sexed; but, so far as I could judge from an examination of the specimens, I concluded that the larger birds with heavier beaks and of a brighter green colour were the males, and the smaller, duller birds the females.

This species concludes the account of the Parrots, and it may be taken as a general, though not invariable, rule that the larger and more brightly coloured birds, with the longer and stronger beaks, are males.   As I have shown, there are exceptions; so that these characters can only be accepted as probable indications of the male sex.   Of course, when putting up pairs for breeding purposes, so long as one associates two birds representing the differing types of character, it matters little which is the male and which the female; so soon as they begin to breed, that will be made manifest.   The main thing is to know what differences to look for.

We now come to the Doves, the sexes of some of which are very difficult indeed to distinguish.   Indeed, in the case of the domesticated Barbary Dove, I doubt if it is possible to tell the sexes, excepting by tedious experimenting (the sexual characters have probably been bred out).   However, I shall do my best to bring together all the information respecting the sexing of the various species of cage Doves that has hitherto been published, or that I can discover by a careful examination of the sexed skins.   It is probable that when accurate measurements are taken of every individual (as is now being done in the United States), the wings of the male birds will be found to differ in outline from those of the females.   It is also likely enough that a comparative study of the colouring of the soft parts will bring to light differences of tint in the irides of the sexes, as in many of the Parrots.   The late Mr Abrahams assured me that the male and female of the Australian Crested Pigeon differed in this respect; but as my supposed pair consisted of two cocks, I was unable to confirm the truth of this statement.

Chapter XXVII.

FRUIT-PIGEONS (*Treronidæ*).

Wedge-tailed Fruit-Pigeon (*Sphenocercus sphenurus*).

The female "differs from the male in being of a darker green, and in having no maroon on the wings and back, which are olive-green, uniform with the rest of the upper parts; there is no rufous tinge on the crown and breast, and the longer under tail-coverts are yellowish-white centred with ashy olive-green" (Salvadori, *Catalogue of Birds*, vol. xxi. p. 9).

Thick-billed Fruit-Pigeon (*Vinago crassirostris*).

Only the male is sexed in the Natural History Museum, but the probable female differs in being smaller and altogether of a deeper colour. There seems to be no reliable difference in the form of the bills, but this seems to be frequently the case among the Doves.

Bare-faced Fruit-Pigeon (*Vinago calva*).

The female is smaller than the male, with an altogether smaller and narrower bill; the naked frontal patch in this sex is more restricted. The plumage of the sexes is similar, but variable, some examples showing more greyish-lavender on the back than others, but whether the differences are local or are due to age I cannot say; they are not sexual.

Delalande's Fruit-Pigeon (*Vinago delalandei*).

The female is smaller than the male. The bills of the sexes vary somewhat, but do not seem to offer reliable sexual differences. As regards plumage, the head and neck of the female are of a more uniform and deeper olive-green than in the male.

Purple-shouldered Fruit-Pigeon (*Crocopus phœnicopterus*).

The female is smaller than the male; the bill variable. According to Count Salvadori, "The female differs from the male in plumage, in that the purple tinge near the bend of the wing is very slightly marked, and the under tail-coverts are slate-grey, more or less mixed with chestnut, in the middle" (*Catalogue of Birds*, vol. xxi. p. 28).

Southern Fruit-Pigeon (*Crocopus chlorogaster*).

The female is slightly the smaller bird; the differences in the bill are unreliable. "The purple tinge near the bend of the wing very slightly marked, and the under tail-coverts of a grey colour in the middle, more or less mixed with chestnut" (Salvadori, *Catalogue of Birds*, vol. xxi. p. 30).

Double-banded Fruit-Pigeon (*Osmotreron bicincta*).

The female is perhaps slightly smaller than the male. "Has the blue of the hind neck of less extent, but darker than the male; the upper surface is more overcast with brownish; the chest wants the lilac and orange bands; under tail-coverts whitish, the inner webs mostly cinnamon, and the bases of the feathers dappled with ashy" (Salvadori, *Catalogue of Birds*, vol. xxi. p. 58).

Parrot Fruit-Pigeon (*Osmotreron vernans*).

"*Female* differs from the male in having the head, neck, and breast green, with a dull yellowish tinge on the forehead, sides of the head, throat, and breast; besides, the under tail-coverts are buffish-white, more or less suffused, generally on the inner web, but sometimes on both, with pale dull cinnamon, which, again, is often freckled or powdered in patches with dark grey or greenish-grey; no grey on the head, no vinous colour round the neck, and no orange patch on the breast" (Salvadori, *Catalogue of Birds*, vol. xxi. p. 62).

The species of *Ptilopus*, on account of their small size, would, I think, be more correctly spoken of as Doves than as pigeons; still, they have always been spoken of as pigeons.

Jambu Fruit-Pigeon (*Ptilopus jambu*).

The female is smaller than the male, and the crown of the head is green, suffused with bluish-lavender instead of petunia-crimson; the stripe on the throat dark cinnamon. Breast, greyish-green, its lower portion greyish-white; abdomen white; under tail-coverts of a paler cinnamon than in the male.

Banded Fruit-Pigeon (*Ptilopus fasciatus*).

The female is smaller than the male; the magenta on the crown without yellow edging at the back; the back of neck and mantle greyish-green, paler than the back; under parts also altogether greener than in the male.

Purple-crowned Fruit-Pigeon (*Ptilopus porphyraceus*).

There seems to be little difference in size between the sexes, but the plumage of the female is altogether much greener than that of the male; apparently the dark green abdominal spot is destitute of a purple tinge, but it is possible that this may prove to be a variable character.

SUPERB FRUIT-PIGEON (*Ptilopus superbus*).

In the female the upper parts, including the crown and back of neck, are green, but with a blue spot on the occiput; the blue spots on the scapulars and inner secondaries are less distinct than in the male, and the blue patch near the bend of the wing is wanting; lower part of throat and breast grey and green without purple at the base of the feathers; no transverse black band below the breast.

BLACK-HEADED FRUIT-PIGEON (*Ptilopus melanocephalus*).

The female is smaller than the male; the throat greyish; the abdomen broadly streaked longitudinally with ashy greyish; the feathers edged with yellow fringes; only the longest of the under tail-coverts crimson, otherwise wholly green.

RED-CROWNED FRUIT-PIGEON (*Alectrœnas pulcherrima*).

The sexes are much alike, but the female is perhaps a trifle smaller; the bill shorter and decidedly broader at base; the blue-black of the plumage is not quite so lustrous, the blue reflections being less pronounced.

PACIFIC FRUIT-PIGEON (*Globicera pacifica*).

The female is smaller than the male, its bill broader at the base. It is possible that in fully adult birds the roughened knob at the base of the bill may be smaller in the female, but it is difficult to judge without knowing the age of the birds.

VINOUS-THROATED FRUIT-PIGEON (*Globicera rufigula*).

There are no females in the Museum series, but it is probable that the female is smaller than the male, and its bill broader at the base.

WHARTON'S FRUIT-PIGEON (*Carpophaga whartoni*).

The Museum example of the male is preserved in spirit, but it is probable that the female is the smaller bird.

RED-NAPED FRUIT-PIGEON (*Carpophaga paulina*).

The female is smaller than the male, its bill perhaps a trifle longer and more slender; the under parts are more uniformly coloured.

BRONZE FRUIT-PIGEON (*Carpophaga œnea*).

The female is smaller than the male, and the plumage of the under parts more uniform in colouring.

BROWN-TAILED FRUIT-PIGEON (*Carpophaga latrans*).

The same note is applicable to this as to the two preceding species, but the sexes in *Carpophaga* are much alike in general appearance.

Nutmeg Fruit-Pigeon (*Myristicivora bicolor*).

The sexes are much alike, but, so far as I could judge, the female would seem to be larger than the male; the bill of the female is certainly more slender.

White Fruit-Pigeon (*Myristicivora luctuosa*).

The sexes differ very little, but the same structural distinctions may be looked for as in the preceding species.

Double-crested Fruit-Pigeon (*Lopholœmus antarcticus*).

"Fleshy part covering the nostrils and at the base of the lower mandible greenish lead colour in the male, and lead colour in the female" (Gould, *Handbook of Birds of Australia*, vol. ii. p. 118).

It is probable that the male is slightly larger than the female, with a slightly better developed crest, but it is difficult to judge from an examination of the dried skins.

Chapter XXVIII.

TYPICAL PIGEONS (*Columbidæ*).

This family includes the Rock-Dove, Stock-Dove, and Ring-Dove (so-called) of the British Islands, but it seems hardly worth while to consider them apart from their foreign relatives.

White-backed Pigeon (*Columba leuconota*).

The sexes are much alike, but the female is perhaps a little smaller, and the grey colouring of its wings and back somewhat duller, the back browner, the nape less white, abdomen smoky rather than pearly ash coloured.

Rock-Pigeon (*Columba livia*).

The female is smaller than the male, and has a narrower bill as viewed in profile, the rosy-violet of the scapulars is less lustrous. Whether any of these characters will be of any value in distinguishing the sexes of the domesticated races is very doubtful.

Stock-Dove (*Columba œnas*).

The female is smaller than the male, its bill when viewed in profile is narrower, the general colouring perhaps a trifle paler, the lower back and rump bluish-ash (less slaty than in the male), the mantle showing less prismatic rosy-lilac, the feathers of the back and inner portion of wings less evidently edged with dusky.

TRIANGULAR-SPOTTED PIGEON (*Columba guinea*).

Only sexed males are recorded in the Catalogue, but, according to Salvadori, the female is similar to the male, though somewhat smaller; it is probable that the bill of the male is heavier when seen in profile.

NAKED-EYED PIGEON (*Columba gymnophthalma*).

Only one example in the Museum: but the same structural differences—that is, in size and character of bill—should be looked for as in most of the species of the genus.

PICAZURO PIGEON (*Columba picazuro*).

Only males are indicated in the Museum Catalogue; therefore look for the same structural differences.

SPOTTED PIGEON (*Columba maculosa*).

The same note applies to this as to the preceding species.

OLIVE PIGEON * (*Columba arquatrix*).

"*Female.*—Somewhat smaller and duller in colour than the male; the vinous-purple colour of the neck more greyish" (Salvadori, *Catalogue of Birds*, vol. xxi. p. 277).

WHITE-CROWNED PIGEON (*Columba leucocephala*).

According to Salvadori, the female is somewhat smaller and duller than the male; "the top of the head, at least in some specimens, tinged with dirty grey."

PORTO RICO PIGEON (*Columba squamosa*).

"*Female.*—Similar to the male, but somewhat smaller and perhaps duller" (Salvadori, *Catalogue of Birds*, vol. xxi. p. 281).

SPECIOUS PIGEON (*Columba speciosa*).

"*Female.*—Differs from the male in being much duller, and principally in having the back, rump, and smaller wing-coverts brown, with no maroon colour" (Salvadori, *Catalogue of Birds*, vol. xxi. p. 283).

CUBAN PIGEON (*Columba inornata*).

The female is smaller and duller in colouring than the male.

RING-TAILED PIGEON (*Columba caribœa*).

The sexes have been stated to be alike, but Count Salvadori seems doubtful of the accuracy of this assertion. Comparing sexes in the Natural History Museum, I noted that the male was slightly

---

* As the Zoological Society gives the same trivial name to this as to the preceding pigeon, I have adopted the name proposed in Stark and Sclater's *Birds of South Africa*, vol. iv. p. 163.

K

larger than the female, brighter in colouring, less smoky in all its tints; the female, sometimes at anyrate, more gravel-reddish on the under surface.

Rufous Pigeon (*Columba rufina*).

"*Female.*—Somewhat duller, and with the chestnut colour of the upper parts less extended on the back and upper wing-coverts " (Salvadori, *Catalogue of Birds*, vol. xxi. p. 288).

Banded Pigeon (*Columba fasciata*).

The female is smaller and duller than the male; "the head and under parts are less vinous and more reddish " (Salvadori, *Catalogue of Birds*, vol. xxi. p. 292).

White-naped Pigeon (*Columba albilinea*).

Only males in the Museum; but Count Salvadori thinks the female is probably similar to the male, but duller; but, he adds, "not without the white nuchal band, as stated by Taczanowski." This is judging by analogy only, but is probably correct.

Araucanian Pigeon (*Columba araucana*).

The female is smaller than the male, and its bill viewed in profile is more slender.

Canarian Pigeon (*Columba laurivora*).

The female is much smaller than the male, and shows more prismatic rosy lilac on the back.

Bolle's Pigeon (*Columba bollei*).

The female is smaller and considerably duller than the male; the prismatic colours on the back of her neck are much less developed, her hinder abdomen is more ashy.

Madeiran Pigeon (*Columba trocax*).

The female is distinctly duller than the male; she shows less prismatic green on the hind neck, and her abdomen is bluer. Count Salvadori notes none of these differences.

Wood Pigeon (*Columba palumbus*).

The female is much smaller than the male, and has a more slender bill (viewed in profile); her back is browner, and she shows less white on the sides of her neck.

White-throated Violet Pigeon (*Columba albigularis*).

Only males are sexed in the Museum, but the female is probably smaller and duller. Some of the unsexed specimens are darker and altogether less red on the under parts than others, but there is no indication as to whether these are sexual differences.

Vinaceous Pigeon (*Columba plumbea*).

According to Salvadori the female is duller than the male and less vinous underneath, often with reddish spots on the nape.

Narrow-barred Pigeon (*Macropygia leptogrammica*).

The female is smaller and duller than the male; she is much less distinctly barred above; below buffish without the lilacine wash on the breast; flanks rust-red; both breast and sides heavily barred with dark brown.

Pheasant-tailed Pigeon (*Macropygia phasianella*).

Count Salvadori says: "Whether the adult female is similar to the adult male, or resembles the young bird, is still doubtful." And yet there is a female from Port Molle which this author records as an adult skin, and which undoubtedly resembles the young bird. I therefore append the Count's description of the latter: "Upper parts chestnut-brown, upper part of the head much redder chestnut, and also the edges of the upper wing-coverts; the sides of the head and neck rufous with brown bars; beneath minutely freckled with dark brown."

Emilian Pigeon (*Macropygia emiliana*).

In the female the mantle is crossed by dusky-bordered cinnamon bars; her throat is paler than in the male, her breast broader, with dusky margins to the feathers in front.

Passenger Pigeon (*Ectopistes migratorius*).

Count Salvadori thus distinguishes the female: "Head, hind neck, back, scapulars, and smaller wing-coverts pale brown; rump and upper tail-coverts grey; sides of the neck glittering with amethystine-purple; throat reddish-white; lower fore-part of the neck and breast pale brown, paler than above, and fading into white on the abdomen and under tail-coverts; median and greater wing-coverts, brownish-grey; the median wing-coverts, the scapulars, and the tertials with black spots, more numerous than in the male; quills brown, the inner primaries dull greyish at the base of the inner web; tail as in the male, but the central feathers have a brown grey tinge" (*Catalogue of Birds*, vol. xxi. p. 371). With regard to the more numerous spots on the wing-coverts, scapulars, and tertials, Charles Otis Whitman observes: "In birds taken at random, I count in the left wing and scapulars 90 checkers in a juvenal, 51 in an adult female, and 25 in an adult male" ("The Problem of the Origin of Species," in *Congress of Arts and Science, Universal Exposition, St Louis*, 1904, vol. v.).

Chapter XXIX.

TURTLE DOVES AND ALLIES (*Peristeridæ*).

THIS family embraces the whole of the Doves and many of the Pigeons; it is therefore convenient to use the subfamilies into which it has been divided.

So-called Ground Doves (*Zenaidinæ*).

These birds, as a matter of fact, rarely visit the ground excepting to feed; they are quite as arboreal in their habits as the majority of the Columbæ. The *Peristerinæ*, *Phabinæ*, and *Geotrygoninæ* are the true Ground Doves and Pigeons. The present subfamily includes birds nearly related to the Turtle Doves.

CAROLINA DOVE (*Zenaidura carolinensis*).

The female is smaller than the male, without the purple tint on the under parts, which are greyish-brown, but paler than the back; the blue on head and neck ill defined and less iridescent.

MARTINICAN DOVE (*Zenaida aurita*).

The female is smaller than the male, more squat in figure, and with smaller purplish-blue patches on the sides of the hind neck.

ZENAIDA DŎVE (*Zenaida amabilis*).

Only males are sexed in the Museum series, but doubtless the female is smaller and less brightly coloured.

BRONZE-NECKED DOVE (*Zenaida auriculata*).

The female is smaller and appears somewhat stouter than the male; she is duller in colour, the vinous tinting replaced by pale dull brown, and the brassy purple-shot patches on the sides of the neck smaller.

Mr Creswell records the breeding of *Z. maculata* in his aviaries (*Avicultural Magazine*, First Series, vol. iii. p. 205), but Count Salvadori refers that bird, as a synonym, to *Z. auriculata*.

GALAPAGAN DOVE (*Nesopelia galapagoensis*).

The female is smaller and paler than the male.

WHITE-WINGED ZENAIDA DOVE (*Melopelia leucoptera*).

The female is rather smaller than the male, and with scarcely a trace of the purplish colour on the crown and nape.

The Typical Turtle Doves (*Turturinæ*).

COMMON TURTLE DOVE (*Turtur turtur*).

"*Female.*—Rather smaller than the male, and the plumage less bright and pure" (Salvadori, *Catalogue of Birds*, vol. xxi. p. 399).

EASTERN TURTLE DOVE (*Turtur orientalis*).

Nearly related to the European Dove; therefore the same differences may be looked for in the sexes.

MAURITIAN TURTLE DOVE (*Turtur picturatus*).

Only sexed females are recorded in the Museum series, but doubtless the males are larger and somewhat brighter in colouring.

ALDABRAN TURTLE DOVE (*Turtur aldabranus*).

The female is "similar to the male, only somewhat smaller" ["Bill, lead colour, with the tip yellowish; feet, flesh colour."— Sclater]; "iris, bright red" (Salvadori, *Catalogue of Birds*, vol. xxi. p. 412).

BARBARY TURTLE DOVE (*Turtur risorius*).

This domesticated race is extremely hard to sex. The male is perhaps a slightly slimmer bird than the female, and his forehead a trifle more prominent; but in pairing them up for breeding I have been so often deceived, and had to revise my decisions, that I have concluded that such differences as existed in the original wild stock have been practically bred out. On one occasion I concluded that I had in one aviary a female and three males. I picked out the former and one of the others and caged them for breeding purposes. Shortly after both laid eggs. I then separated them and substituted a second supposed male, and again both laid. I actually had one male and three females, yet by their actions, their quarrelsome behaviour, and their eagerness to breed, I was completely hoodwinked.

HALF-COLLARED TURTLE DOVE (*Turtur semitorquatus*).

The sexes are a good deal alike, but the male is distinctly paler (more ashy) on the forehead than the female; so that, seeing the two together in an aviary, there is no difficulty in distinguishing it at a glance.

DOUBLE-RINGED TURTLE DOVE (*Turtur bitorquatus*).

Count Salvadori describes the female as "like the male," but I have no doubt that in the living bird the forehead is paler than in the male. Such differences are less pronounced in the dead skins.

CAPE TURTLE DOVE (*Turtur capicola*).

I have no doubt that the same note applies to this as to the preceding species, although Stark and Sclater agree with Salvadori in stating that the sexes are alike. In living Doves also, the female almost always has a more squat, heavy appearance than the male.

Vinaceous Turtle Dove (*Turtur vinaceus*).

Only one male is sexed in the Museum, but in picking out a female I should look for the same differences indicated for the preceding three species.

Ruddy Turtle Dove (*Turtur humilis*).

"*Female.*—General colour pale brown, but the lower parts vinous-grey where vinous-red in the male. There is a black collar as in the male, but edged above with whitish-grey" (Salvadori, *Catalogue of Birds*, vol. xxi. p. 435).

Chinese Turtle Dove (*Turtur chinensis*).

The sexes are much alike, but the female is slightly smaller and less alert in appearance.

Necklaced Dove (*Turtur tigrinus*).

The same note applies to this as to the preceding species.

Spotted Turtle Dove (*Turtur suratensis*).

The female is a trifle smaller than the male, and less alert in appearance, as in the two preceding allied species.

Senegal Turtle Dove (*Turtur senegalensis*).

Also known as the Cambayan Turtle Dove. The female is smaller and duller in colouring than the male.

Aberrant Turtle Doves (*Geopeliinæ*).

Bar-shouldered Dove (*Geopelia humeralis*).

The female is slightly smaller than the male (but, unfortunately, the males also vary a good deal in size); her breast, however, is of a darker and duller grey than in the male.

Peaceful Dove (*Geopelia tranquilla*).

The female is a smaller, less slender, and alert bird than the male, but the sexes are extremely alike in the skin.

Zebra Dove (*Geopelia striata*).

The female is smaller than the male, and shows less reddish tinting on the crown.

Mauge's Dove (*Geopelia maugœi*).

The female is smaller and less slender in appearance than the male.

Diamond Dove (*Geopelia cuneata*).

"*Female.*—Smaller than the male; back of the head, neck, and upper surface browner, and the spots on the wings larger" (Salvadori, *Catalogue of Birds*, vol. xxi. p. 463).

SCALY DOVE (*Scardafella squamosa*).

Mr Seth-Smith, who bred this species in his aviaries some years
ago, did not say how he distinguished the sexes; but Dr Russ, who
bred it many years before, says: "The female can only be
distinguished in this respect, that in all its markings, and particularly
in the rose-coloured ones, it appears duller" (*Die Fremdländischen
Stubenvögel*, vol. ii. p. 785). In some which I saw soon after their
importation, it struck me that the scaling on the breast was better
marked in the male than in the female, but this character may
perhaps be variable.

Metal-spotted Turtle Doves (*Peristerinæ*).

STEEL-BARRED DOVE (*Columbula picui*).

The female is distinctly smaller than the male, and her bill
viewed in profile is more slender; the upper parts are paler, browner,
without the bluish-grey tint of the cock bird, the breast browner
with less of the rosy tinting of the male, and the sides of the
abdomen, though paler, are of the same sordid tint, but in this last
detail some males are indistinguishable from the hens.

PASSERINE DOVE (*Chamœpelia passerina*).

There are many local races of this species, which differ from one
another in the colouring of the soft parts and the amount of rose
colour in their plumage.* That most frequently imported as a
cage-bird differs sexually as follows:—The male is larger than the
female, has a stouter bill, has better defined breast markings and a
delicate rosy tint over that part of the body. There may be other
slight differences, but my male bird is still living, and therefore not
easily compared with his dead wife, and to compare many skins
from various localities is confusing.

TALPACOTI DOVE (*Chamœpelia talpacoti*).

Dr Russ thus distinguishes the female from the male: "Female
greyer, the shoulder-bars narrower and less distinct" (*Die Fremd
ländischen Stubenvögel*, vol. ii. p. 787). Salvadori describes "a
brownish tinge on the mantle." *C. minuta* is also said to have
been imported; sexes very different.

CINEREOUS DOVE (*Peristera cinerea*).

"*Female.*—Upper parts brown, almost cinnamon on the upper
tail-coverts, paler on the forehead; spots on the upper wing-
coverts and inner secondaries brown-cinnamon, the larger ones
on the median and greater wing-coverts bounded behind with a
light line; throat whitish, lower fore-neck and breast pale brown,

* For instance, Count Salvadori says: "*Female.*—With little or none of the
purplish-red"; but the form most imported shows only delicate rosy pink on the
breast of the male.

changing into grey on the rest of the lower parts ; under tail-coverts greyish-cinnamon ; under wing-coverts grey ; central tail-feathers brown-cinnamon ; lateral rectrices black, but the inner ones tinged with rufous on the outer webs, outer pair edged with rufous on the outer web" (Salvadori, *Catalogue of Birds*, vol. xxi. p. 492).

Geoffroy's Dove (*Peristera geoffroyi*).

" *Female.*—Reddish-brown, paler on the forehead, throat, and abdomen, changing into fawn colour on the vent and under tail-coverts ; three oblique bands on the wings, a very narrow deep blue one on the smaller wing-coverts, the other two on the median and greater wing-coverts of a chestnut colour, and edged behind with a narrow band of fawn colour ; bastard wing, primary coverts, and under wing-coverts blackish-brown ; quills brown, with narrow reddish edges ; two central tail-feathers reddish-brown, the lateral ones greyish towards the base, black about the middle, and reddish-fawn colour at the tip" (Salvadori, *Catalogue of Birds*, vol. xxi. pp. 494, 495).

Black-winged Dove (*Metriopelia melanoptera*).

The female differs from the male in its greyish-brown under parts without rosy tint ; chin and middle of abdomen almost white.

Chapter XXX.

BRONZE-WINGS (*Phabinæ*).

Harlequin Dove (*Œna capensis*).

"The female has no black on the head or breast, the forehead and breast being white to mauve-grey ; the crown and nape are brown like the back ; the white on the outer pair of tail-feathers also is more developed, especially on the outer web ; bill blackish ; feet dark purplish-grey" (Stark and Sclater, *Birds of South Africa*, vol. iv. p. 175).

Tambourine Dove (*Tympanistria tympanistria*).

"In the female the white of the face and under parts is tinged with dusky ; the wing spots are black, and not metallic" (Stark and Sclater, *Birds of South Africa*, vol. iv. p. 179). In addition to the above, the female is slightly smaller and more squat than the male.

Emerald Dove (*Chalcopelia chalcospila*).

The female is smaller and paler than the male, and has a less alert and more squat appearance.

BLUE-SPOTTED DOVE (*Chalcopelia afra*).

"The sexes seem to be practically alike, the only observable difference being the barely paler colour and slightly smaller size of the female" (Oberholzer, *Proc. United States Nat. Mus.*, vol. xxviii. p. 844).

As Professor Oberholzer states, this and the preceding species, until quite recently, were believed · to be identical; indeed, they were frequently regarded as sexes, but as this American author observes : "Aside from an interesting difference in habits noted by Mr Erlanger—*chalcospila* living among the acacias on the plains, and *afra* more confined to the forests—these two species may be distinguished as follows: *Chalcopelia afra* is much larger; it has blue or purple instead of bright green metallic spots on the inner wing-coverts; the bill is yellow instead of almost black; the brown area of the entire upper surface is decidedly more rufescent; and the chin, as well as the cheeks, flanks, and abdomen are strongly tinged with buff." As I have living specimens of both species, I am able to confirm these distinctions : of *C. chalcospila* I have both sexes, and of *C. afra* a male.

MAIDEN DOVE (*Calopelia puella*).

"The female is perhaps a trifle smaller than the male, has a rather less prominent forehead, and is much less alert and heavier in her movements" (Butler, *Avicultural Magazine*, N.S., vol. iv. p. 252).
Inserted out of its natural position in the Museum Catalogue.

AUSTRALIAN GREEN-WINGED DOVE (*Chalcophaps chrysochlora*).

The female is smaller and duller than the male, less vinous in tint; the white on the shoulder of the wing is wanting, or only represented by an indistinct greyish patch; under tail-coverts ruddy brown; tail above chestnut-brown, the lateral feathers with a black subterminal band; outer tail-feathers grey, as in the male.

CHRISTMAS ISLAND GREEN-WINGED DOVE (*Chalcophaps natalis*).

"The female has the upper tail-coverts of a pure cinnamon colour, like the central tail-feathers; also the under tail-coverts are of a cinnamon colour, without blackish tips" (Salvadori, *Catalogue of Birds*, vol. xxi. p. 520). Doubtless this sex is also smaller and less elegantly formed than the male.

INDIAN GREEN-WINGED DOVE (*Chalcophaps indica*).

"*Female.*—Forehead dull grey, and the supercilium narrower; occiput, nape, and upper back, brown; under parts reddish-brown, minutely speckled with grey points; smaller wing-coverts on the shoulders brown, with scarcely any paler tips; four central tail-feathers brown-black, next two pairs tinged with rufous chestnut towards the base; two outer feathers as in the male" (Salvadori, *Catalogue of Birds*, vol. xxi. p. 517).

Bronze-winged Pigeon (*Phaps chalcoptera*).

The female is without the conspicuous buff frontal patch of the male, but has a defined white streak running below the eye and over the ear-coverts nearly as in the male; the general plumage is rather duller, without purplish band on the crown and sides of the occiput; edges of the feathers of the upper parts broader and reddish-grey; breast less vinous, greyer, the feathers edged with

BRONZE-WINGED PIGEON.
(From a Photograph by Miss Alderson.)

brownish. I have not noticed any difference in the metallic spots such as Count Salvadori mentions.

Brush Bronze-winged Pigeon (*Phaps elegans*).

"The female differs in having all her markings duller and less distinct; the breast and under parts dull brownish-grey" (Seth-Smith, *Avicultural Magazine*, N.S., vol. ii. p. 266).

Harlequin Bronze-winged Pigeon (*Histriophaps histrionica*).

"*Female.*—No white on the forehead, which is sandy-rufous, like the upper parts; ear-coverts and throat dull blackish; gorget and a patch below the ear-coverts whitish-buff; crop region pale sandy brown; tips of the primaries and lateral tail feathers whitish-buff" (Salvadori, *Catalogue of Birds*, vol. xxi. pp. 529, 530).

Partridge Bronze-winged Pigeon (*Geophaps scripta*).

According to Salvadori, the female only differs from the male in being smaller, but doubtless in the living birds other distinctions might be detected.

Plumed Ground Dove (*Lophophaps plumifera*).

It is possible that all the specimens recorded under this name as having been imported may belong to the following species, as those which reached London in 1904, according to Mr Seth-Smith, certainly did; the female is slightly smaller than the male.

White-bellied Ground Dove (*Lophophaps leucogaster*).

"The sexes are alike in plumage, the male being perhaps a shade larger than the female. It is about eight inches in length" (Seth-Smith, *Avicultural Magazine*, N.S., vol v. p. 54).

Crested Pigeon (*Ocyphaps lophotes*).

Female rather smaller than the male, and, if the late Mr Abrahams' statement is correct, differing in its paler irides. My birds proved to be two cocks.

Mixed Types (*Geotrygoninæ*).

This subfamily includes first some aberrant types related to the *Zenaidinæ* (Turtle Doves of a kind) from the New World; then a number of more or less terrestrial and bulky birds (some of them vaguely resembling Game birds) from Malaysia, the Moluccas, and Australia; and lastly the strange Blue-headed Pigeon from the West Indies. This collection appears to be hopelessly unnatural.

Rufous-necked Wood Dove (*Haplopelia larvata*).

"The female is slightly duller in colour and smaller in size' (Stark and Sclater, *Birds of South Africa*, vol. iv. p. 183). "Greener and less coppery-red on the hind neck" (Salvadori, *Catalogue of Birds*, vol. xxi. p. 541). Why Messrs Stark and Sclater call this "Lemon Dove" is not clear, as it is neither lemon-coloured nor does it appear to frequent lemon trees.

For the species of *Leptoptila* the Museum Catalogue records sexual differences in very few instances, but one can always distinguish the sexes in life by careful observation.

Red-underwinged Dove (*Leptoptila rufaxilla*).

Although Count Salvadori merely says of the female "similar to the male," I have no doubt that her forehead is less white, her general plumage a trifle duller; and, if she is not smaller, I am sure she is less alert in appearance when alive.

Rufous Dove (*Leptoptila reichenbachii*).

Only a male is sexed in the Museum, therefore the same differences may be looked for as indicated for the preceding species.

Orange-winged Dove (*Leptoptila ochroptera*).

Here, again, the same sexual differences should be looked for; features not readily discerned in dried skins are quite apparent in living birds.

White-fronted Dove (*Leptoptila jamaicensis*).

It is much to be regretted that Miss Alderson and others who have bred this species, and evidently were able to recognise the sexes

WHITE-FRONTED DOVE.
(*From a Photograph by Miss Alderson.*)

in life, have not recorded any sexual differences. In the Museum there are no sexed specimens, and it is some time since I last saw a living pair; but I am almost sure the forehead of the male was whiter and the entire bird a trifle larger than the female.

Wells' Ground Dove (*Leptoptila wellsi*).

"The female is very similar, the forehead less white, and the colouring generally, perhaps, a trifle duller" (Butler, *Foreign Bird-Keeping*, part ii. p. 97).

I hardly know why this should have been called a Ground Dove; it is not more so than the *Zenaidinæ*. My widowed hen during the last year of her life seemed to hint at her relationship to the true Turtle Doves by trying to get at some in the next aviary, yet when I turned one in with her they never paired up, and she continued to lay clear eggs incessantly for a whole year and longer.

RED GROUND DOVE (*Geotrygon montana*).

"*Female.*—Upper parts dark olive, with a golden lustre; forehead and cheeks rufous, the latter bounded below by an olive band; throat whitish-rufous; lower throat and breast olive-brown; lower breast and abdomen buffy, with a more or less distinct brown tinge; quills brown, with the base of the inner webs cinnamon; tail olive-brown above, with a rufous tinge towards the base of the feathers, very distinct on the under surface of the tail" (Salvadori, *Catalogue of Birds*, vol. xxi. p. 569).

MOUSTACHE GROUND DOVE (*Geotrygon mystacea*).

Count Salvadori only describes the male, yet only indicates a sexed female in the Collection. It is probable that the male is larger and brighter in colouring than the female.

MOUNTAIN WITCH GROUND DOVE (*Geotrygon cristata*).

Only a male is sexed and described in the Museum Catalogue.

CHAPTER XXXI.

GROUND AND NICOBAR PIGEONS.

THE Pigeons which follow, although also referred in the Museum Catalogue of Birds to the *Geotrygoninæ*, are so utterly dissimilar, both in appearance and habits, to those previously noted, that I think it better to place them in another chapter.

BLEEDING-HEART PIGEON
(*Phlogœnas luzonica*).

The female is distinctly smaller than the male, and has a more slender bill when viewed in profile; the forehead is much less white, more bluish-ash than in the male, and the blood-stain on the breast covers only half the extent of that in her mate; the flank feathers are slightly browner, and show ill-defined, darker transverse bars, owing to the tips of the fringes being more evidently browner. The

THE BLEEDING-HEART PIGEON.
(*From a Photograph by Miss Alderson.*)

sexes have been described as similar, only the female a little smaller; but careful comparison will show that in this, as in other species so described, real colour differences do exist.

Bartlett's Ground Pigeon (*Phlogœnas crinigera*).

The female is smaller and has a slightly more slender bill than the male when viewed in profile; its general plumage is a good deal like that of the male, but the crown of its head is of a duller and darker green.

Stair's Ground Pigeon (*Phlogœnas stairi*).

The female is smaller than the male, and has a shorter bill; the forehead and breast wholly dull pale chocolate, back of crown darker; back and wings washed with olive in place of the magenta

HEADS OF MALE AND FEMALE OF THE BLEEDING-HEART PIGEON.

on the male; abdomen brownish-ash, with no defined broad dark purplish-chocolate band between it and the breast; tail also paler than in the male, the lateral feathers redder and with a subterminal brown bar.

Of the following large species I unfortunately omitted to commit notes to paper when my pair was alive and in my possession, and as the examples in the Museum Collection are unfortunately not sexed, and no difference is recorded in the Catalogue, I shall have to trust to my memory: whether the differences of which I made a mental note are all constant or not I cannot say, therefore can only record what I observed in my own birds, being assured that at least some of the differences will prove to be constant.

WONGA-WONGA PIGEON (*Leucosarcia picata*).

The female of my pair stood higher from the ground than the male, and when roosting did not lean forward at an angle, with the tail pointed obliquely upwards and lifting rhythmically up and down (I believe this was intended as an invitation to the hen bird *). Her forehead is not of so pure a white, and is more or less stained with brown at the back. The white bands extending from the shoulders across the sides of the breast were broader in my hen bird than in the cock, and the spots on the under parts were more numerous, and frequently divided into pairs, between which the feather-shaft passed; this last character is, I think, more likely to be variable than the others which I have mentioned.

BLUE-HEADED PIGEON (*Starnœnas cyanocephala*).

Of this beautiful species the Natural History Museum only possesses one stuffed example from Cuba and one skin labelled "W. Indies," received from the Zoological Society's Gardens. They are probably both males, and only that sex is described in the Museum Catalogue. I think it likely that the female would be a trifle smaller, and duller in all her colours.

Subfamily **Calœnadinæ.**

This group comprises the handsome Nicobar Island Pigeon and the smaller Pelew Island Pigeon, curious Vulturine-looking birds which seem to exhibit some relationship to the Guinea-fowls.

NICOBAR PIGEON (*Calœnas nicobarica*).

The female is smaller than the male, and does not sit so erect on the perch; her bill, when viewed in profile, is seen to be much more slender, and the frontal knob at the base of the upper mandible is small and little developed; her plumage above is less varied with metallic golden copper, and below shows rather less of the gleaming emerald green of the cock bird; the hackle feathers from the back of the neck are shorter.

The families *Gouridœ* (or Crown Pigeons) and *Didunculidœ* (or little Dodos) can hardly be regarded as cage-birds. Of the former, visitors to our Gardens will be familiar with two species—*Goura coronata* and *G. victoriœ*, majestic-looking birds from two to three feet long, strutting about their aviaries and looking as unlike an ordinary Dove as possible. Of the latter, the only representative is the Tooth-billed Pigeon (*Didunculus strigirostris*), an extremely rarely imported bird, a foot long, of which the Museum possesses no skin sexed as a female. The sexes are said to be alike, but there is

---

* I feel sure of this now, as I have seen the cock Australian Green-winged Dove do the same thing before pursuing his mate.

no doubt that an examination and comparison of living male and female would reveal differences, even if none could be discovered in the dried skins.

As I do not regard the Game-birds, Plovers, Waders, or true Aquatic birds as cage-birds, this will bring to a close my notes on sexual characters. Much more study is needed to bring our knowledge of even these external characters to anything approaching perfection, but as a step in the right direction I hope my efforts will be useful to bird students, whether aviculturists or cabinet-workers.

INDEX TO ENGLISH NAMES.

INDEX TO SCIENTIFIC NAMES.

"The Feathered World,"
"Canary & Cage-Bird Life," } 9 Arundel Street, London, W.C.
(M. & E.)

CANARY & CAGE BIRD LIFE